Great HANDEL choruses

17 choruses for *mixed voices* *from* Handel's sacred works

Selected *with introductory notes*

Novello

Orchestral material for all the pieces
in this volume is available for hire,
as separate items, from the Publisher

NOV078419
ISBN 07119-9588-5

*Cover illustration: The Handel Monument, Westminster Abbey
by Louis-François Roubiliac (1705-1762)
© Dean and Chapter of Westminster
Photograph of Brian Kay © BBC*

Published in Great Britain by Novello Publishing Limited
Head office: 14-15 Berners Street, London W1T 3LJ
Tel +44 (0) 7612 7400 Fax +44 (0)20 7612 7546

Sales and Hire: Music Sales Distribution Centre
Newmarket Road, Bury St. Edmunds, Suffolk IP33 3YB
Tel +44 (0)1284 702600 Fax +44 (0)1284 768301

e-mail: music@musicsales.co.uk

Music setting by Stave Origination

www.musicsalesclassical.com

"He is the master of us all". So said Joseph Haydn after a performance of *Messiah* at Westminster Abbey in 1791 had moved him to tears of admiration. Indeed, Haydn was so overwhelmed by the power of the music and the audience's reaction to it that, at an age when most people would be considering retirement, he resolved to devote the rest of his life to writing major choral works, completing *The Creation, The Seasons, The Seven Last Words of Christ on the Cross* and six glorious settings of the Mass between the ages of 63 and 70. What was it about Handel's commitment to the Oratorio that so inspired the man who was by then the most famous composer in Europe? And what is it that still encourages us, two centuries later, to turn to Handel whenever two or three hundred are gathered together for a good sing? - or in these days of 'historical awareness', smaller numbers with more vocal muscle and greater technical skills?

Leigh Hunt summed him up like this: "Handel was the Jupiter of music; his hallelujahs open the heavens. He utters the word 'Wonderful' as if all their trumpets spoke together. And then, when he comes to earth, to make love amidst nymphs and shepherds ... his strains drop milk and honey, and his love is the youthfulness of the Golden Age." And Edward Fitzgerald, writing in 1847, claimed that "Handel never gets out of his wig, that is, out of his age: his Hallelujah Chorus is a chorus, not of angels, but of well-fed earthly choristers, ranged tier above tier in a Gothic cathedral, with princes for audience, and their military trumpets flourishing over the full volume of the organ." *Zadok the Priest* has been sung at every coronation since that of George II in 1727, and countless annual performances of *Messiah* have, as Charles Burney claimed as long ago as 1781, "fed the hungry, clothed the naked, fostered the orphan, and enriched succeeding managers of the Oratorios, more than any single production in this or any country".

Look beyond those two works and the sheer quantity of Handel's choral music is staggering - not to mention the quality, which for singers and audiences alike creates a sense of vocal, emotional and spiritual uplift that is second to none. The notes are relatively easy to learn - except when Handel makes one of his many harmonic twists or turns in order to underline the drama. But the sheer number of those notes is so great that considerable vocal stamina is required - and richly rewarded in rehearsal and performance. When the music of celebration is asked for, then Handel is indeed 'the master of us all' - more often than not in the key of D major, so that the best parts of the vocal range can be exploited, and the trumpets can sound to their brightest and best. No wonder in the golden age of choral societies, it was Handel's music which featured so prominently - as indeed it still does and no doubt always will. The selection of choruses in this volume merely scratches the surface of Handel's remarkable output, and should serve as an introduction to one man's world of choral music that stretches far beyond *Messiah.*

Brian Kay.

Acis and Galatea / Semele
Happy we / Happy shall we be

Two 'happy' choruses find Handel at his most appropriately cheerful. He wrote the pastoral masque ***Acis and Galatea*** in 1718 during his tenure as Court Composer to the Earl of Carnarvon - later Duke of Chandos. It quickly became one of the most popular of all Handel's works, with at least seventy performances in eight revivals during his lifetime. It is a love story, set in blissful Arcadian surroundings where nymphs and shepherds 'dance and sport the hours away'. Their joy is interrupted by the monster Polyphemus whose love for Galatea results in his killing Acis - his rival for her affections. The chorus plays a vital role: it sets the scene, watches and reflects, and in the end takes part in the action. The duet and chorus ***Happy we*** ends part one, as Acis and Galatea are united in their love, unaware of the drama to come. No such drama threatens the final chorus of ***Semele***. Charles Jennens - the irascible collaborator who provided Handel with the text of *Messiah* - dismissed *Semele* as "No Oratorio, but a bawdy opera ... an English opera, but called *by fools* an Oratorio and performed as such at Covent Garden". It concerns the love affair between Jupiter and Semele, and what happens when a mortal tries to assume the status of a god. Semele's eventual demise clears the way for her sister Ino to marry the man Semele had deserted when she fell for Jupiter, and this final chorus celebrates the birth of Bacchus - arising as a phoenix from Semele's ashes, and crowning forever the joys of love.

Alexander's Feast
The many rend the skies / Your voices tune, and raise them high

Handel's ***Alexander's Feast***, which is based on Dryden's 1697 ode for St. Cecilia's Day, is subtitled 'The Power of Music' and it represents his first collaboration with a major English poet, in a work which is technically neither opera nor oratorio, though it could work perfectly well as either. And as it is the overwhelming potency of music that concerns us here, it is hardly surprising that Handel should have risen to the occasion with some of his finest arias and choruses. ***Your voices tune, and raise them high*** ends the ode in praise of the patron saint of music, while ***The many rend the skies*** forms part of the celebrations at Alexander's Feast, reminding us that 'love was crowned, but music won the cause'.

Dixit Dominus
Gloria Patri

Dixit dominus is the opening psalm for festal vespers and Handel's setting dates from the beginning of the eighteenth century when, as a young man in his early twenties, he was living in Rome. It has boundless youthful energy, strikingly original use of harmony and string writing which echoes the Italian *concerto grosso* style pioneered in Rome by Corelli. The choral writing of the final ***Gloria patri*** is also distinctly instrumental in style, building to a massive climax through use of the plainsong melody against exhilarating semiquaver runs in all five parts - including high lying soprano lines which cover the range from low d to high B♭. This closing chorus stands well on its own, but inevitably works best as a suitably glorious conclusion to a thrilling work, in which the rewards from singing overwhelm by far the effort required.

Israel in Egypt

The people shall hear / Sing ye to the Lord

Israel in Egypt is the most popular of Handel's great choral works after *Messiah*, largely because it is such a tremendous sing for the chorus. There are relatively few solos and no named characters, as so much of the action is declaimed by the choir - double chorus as often as not, and containing some of Handel's finest choral writing. ***The people shall hear*** is a powerful and profoundly moving expression of the exiles' longing for home. The drama begins immediately with the dotted accompaniment figure creating an awesome atmosphere. Echoes of 'He was wounded' from *Messiah* are clearly heard in the setting of the words *Sorrow shall take hold of them.* The final section *They shall be as still as a stone till thy people pass over, O Lord* is Handel the choral composer at the very peak of his powers. ***Sing ye to the Lord*** is the oratorio's closing chorus - a great hymn of triumph as the people celebrate the overthrow of their pursuers and the Glory of God.

Judas Maccabaeus

See the conqu'ring hero comes / Sing unto God / Rejoice, O Judah

Judas Maccabaeus was composed in celebration of the victorious conclusion to the battle of Culloden in 1746, and nowhere is the emotional impact of victory more tellingly expressed than in the chorus ***See, the conqu'ring hero comes.*** It is one of Handel's best-known choruses, and it forms part of the celebrations which conclude the third part of the Oratorio, as in turn, the youths, the virgins, and the Israelites welcome victorious Judas. The middle section, for two sopranos, is often sung by solo voices. This hymn-like chorus is followed by ***Sing unto God***, as the celebrations continue, and ***Rejoice, O Judah*** concludes the oratorio in a final burst of triumphal rejoicing.

Messiah

For unto us / Hallelujah / Worthy is the lamb, Amen

These are three of the most familiar and best-loved of all Handel's choruses, and with good reason. ***For unto us a child is born*** is part of the Christmas section of ***Messiah*** and explains the reason for the 'great light' which the birth of the saviour sheds on those who walked in darkness. The mighty ***Hallelujah Chorus*** is so often heard out of context that it is easy to overlook its immense importance as the climax to part two of the oratorio. That second part follows the story of Christ's passion, scourging, crucifixion, death, resurrection and ascension into heaven and this triumphant chorus celebrates the ultimate victory over sin. On completing this chorus, Handel is reputed to have said "I did think I did see all heaven before me, and the great God himself". ***Worthy is the lamb*** represents the ultimate acclamation of the Messiah, and the final ***Amen Chorus***, with its contrapuntal grandeur, is a masterpiece of consummation.

Samson

Let the bright seraphim / Let their celestial concerts all unite (Samson)

The beginning of the 1740s saw Handel at his most prodigiously productive in the field of oratorio. He completed *Saul, Israel in Egypt, L'Allegro, Messiah, Samson* and *Semele* within five years. ***Samson*** tells the story of the strong man's degradation, his determination to prove himself one more time, and his final act of superhuman strength - reducing the temple to rubble and killing himself and his enemies in its ruins. The news of this remarkable feat brings forth lamentation, but is followed by the call, not to lament but to sing the praises of Samson's eternal fame. At this point - the end of the oratorio - the aria and final chorus requires that the bright seraphim blow their trumpets in Samson's honour and all their celestial concerts unite, ever to sing his praise in endless morn of light.

Solomon

Music, spread thy voice around / Praise the Lord with harp and tongue

Handel's 1748 oratorio ***Solomon*** may well be best known for the orchestral sinfonia which begins Part III - the so-called 'Arrival of the Queen of Sheba' - but its fame should really lie in the remarkable strength of its choral writing. The plot concerns the wisdom of Solomon, and this is portrayed most tellingly in the central section, where he is called upon to pass judgement on two harlots, each of whom claims parentage of a baby. But it is also to do with making a political point about the splendours of the Court, and the power of music to enrich its life. When the Queen of Sheba has been welcomed, she is then serenaded with music in its various forms - to calm the fevered brow, to move and shake, to draw a tear, and to restore the mind to peace – ***Music, spread thy voice around***. And the oratorio ends with the double chorus of celebration - ***Praise the Lord with harp and tongue*** - just one of seven choruses in eight parts, to which Handel added five five-part choruses and just one for four voices.

Coronation Anthem

Zadok the Priest

This is the most famous of all coronation anthems - composed for the anointing of George II in 1727, and sung at every coronation service in London since then. It is richly scored for both voices and instruments, and works equally well with a small church choir or a large choral society - and indeed with anything in between. The chorus's massive first entry - after the gradual build-up which precedes it - is one of the most dramatic outbursts in all choral music, and having reached that glorious moment, Handel then retains the sense of excitement right through to the final *Alleluia, Amen.* If a choir is too small to divide all the parts satisfactorily, then it is possible to perform this anthem omitting the second alto and first bass parts.

HAPPY WE

(Air)

from *Acis and Galatea*

John Gay and others
after Ovid

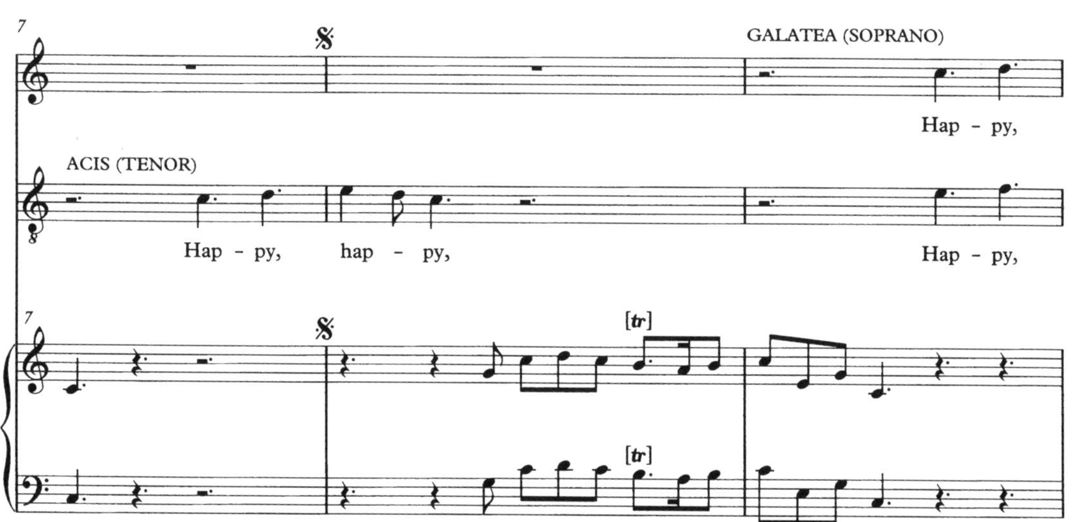

10
hap - py,
hap - py, hap - py, hap - py, we, hap - py, hap - py, hap - py,
hap - py,
hap - py, hap - py, hap - py,
[tr]
[tr]
p
13
we, hap - - - - - - py we, hap - -
we, hap - - - - - py, hap - py we, hap - -
16
- py, hap - - - py, hap - - - - - - - - -
- py, hap - - - py, hap - - - - - - - - -
f
p

19
- - - py, hap - py, hap - py we,
- py, hap - py, hap - py, hap - py we,
19
[tr]
f
[tr]
22
hap - py, hap - py, hap - py, hap - py, hap - py we, hap -
hap - py, hap - py, hap - py,
22
[tr]
[tr]
p
25
- py we, hap - - - - - - - - - - -
hap - py, hap - py we, hap - - - - - - - - - -
25

28
- py, hap - py we, hap - - py, hap -
- py, hap-py, hap - py___ we, hap - - py, hap -
28
[tr]
[tr]
f
[tr]
[tr]

31
- - - - py, hap - py we.
- - - py, hap-py, hap - py___ we.
31
[tr]
[f]
[tr]

34
[tr]
[tr]

(37a) 1.
2.
(37b)
(38)
What
joys___ I feel,
of all
What charms_ I see,
[p]
Fine
segue chorus
40
youth, thou dear - est boy.___
Thou all___ my___ bliss, thou
of all nymphs, thou bright-est fair.___
Thou all___ my___ bliss, thou
43
all___ my___ joy,
Thou all___ my___ bliss,___ thou___ all_______ my joy.
What
all___ my___ joy,
Thou all___ my___ bliss,___ thou___ all_______ my joy.

46
joys I feel,
of all youth, thou dear - est boy.
What charms I see,
of all
49
Thou all my bliss, thou all my joy, thou
nymphs, thou bright - est fair. Thou all my bliss, thou all my joy, thou
52
D.S. al Fine
all my bliss, thou all my joy.
all my bliss, thou all my joy.
Hap - py,
[tr]
f
tr

HAPPY WE

(Chorus)

from *Acis and Galatea*

6
hap - py, hap - py, hap - py we; what joys
hap - py, hap - py, hap - pywe; what joys I feel, what
hap - py, hap - py, hap - py we; what joys
hap - py, hap - py, hap - pywe; what joys I feel, what
6
9
I feel, what charms I see, what charms I see, what
joys I feel, what charms I see, what charms I see, what
I feel, what charms I see, what charms I see, what
joys I feel, what charms I see, what
9

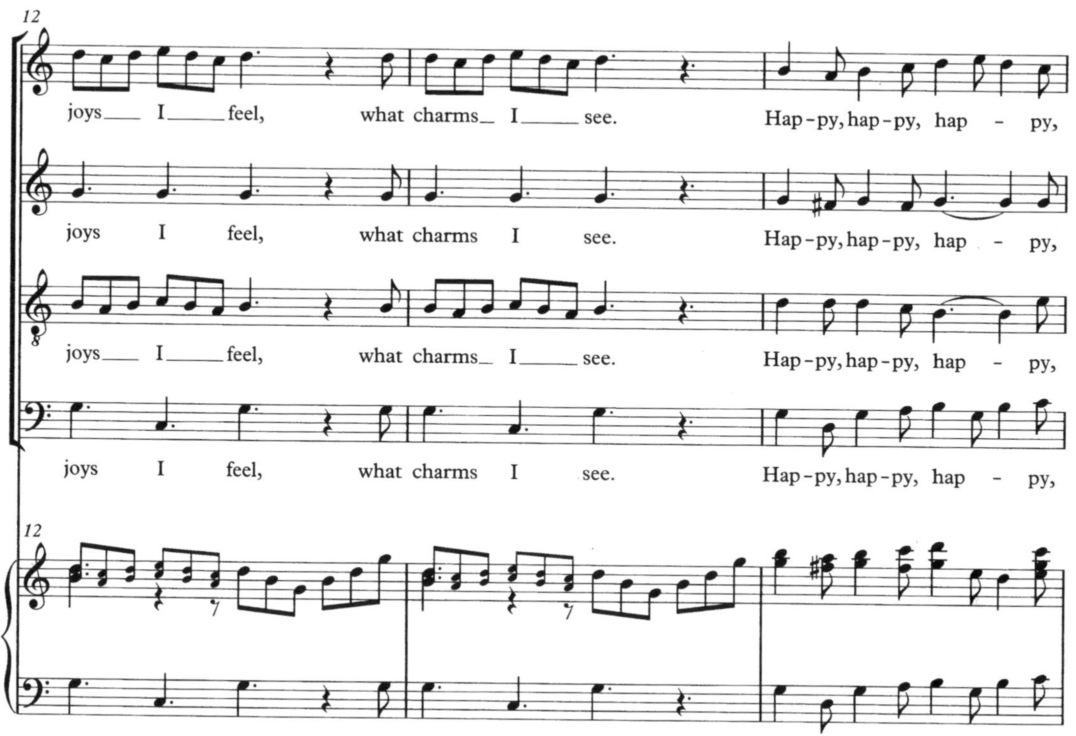
12
joys___ I___ feel, what charms_ I___ see. Hap-py, hap-py, hap - py,
joys I feel, what charms I see. Hap-py, hap-py, hap - py,
joys___ I___ feel, what charms_ I___ see. Hap-py, hap-py, hap - py,
joys I feel, what charms I see. Hap-py, hap-py, hap - py,
12

15
A
hap-py we, hap - py, hap - py hap - py we; what
hap-py we, hap - py, hap - py hap - py we; what
hap-py we, hap - py, hap - py hap - py we; what
hap-py we, hap - py, hap - py hap - py we; what
15
A

18
joys I feel, what charms I see, what
joys I feel, what joys I feel, what charms I see, what
joys I feel, what joys I feel, what charms I see, what
joys I feel, what joys I feel, what charms
18

21
charms I see, what joys I feel, what charms I see.
charms I see, what joys I feel, what charms I see.
charms I see, what joys I feel, what charms I see.
I see, what joys I feel, what charms I see.
21

24
Hap - py, hap - py, hap - py, hap - py we,
Hap - py, hap - py, hap - py, hap - - py we,
Hap - py, hap - py, hap - py, hap - - py we,
Hap - py, hap - py, hap - py, hap - py we,
24
[tr]
[tr]
26
hap - py, hap - py, hap - py, hap - py we.
hap - py, hap - py, hap - py, hap - py we.
hap - py, hap - py, hap - py, hap - py we.
hap - py, hap - py, hap - py, hap - py we.
26

THE MANY REND THE SKIES

from *Alexander's Feast*

John Dryden

15
with loud ap - plause,
with loud ap -
with_ loud ap - plause,
with loud ap -
with loud ap - plause,
with loud ap -
with loud ap - plause,
with loud ap -
15
19
- plause,
with loud
- plause,
with loud
- plause,
with loud
- plause,
with loud
19

23
ap - plause,
ap - plause,
ap - plause,
ap - plause,
23

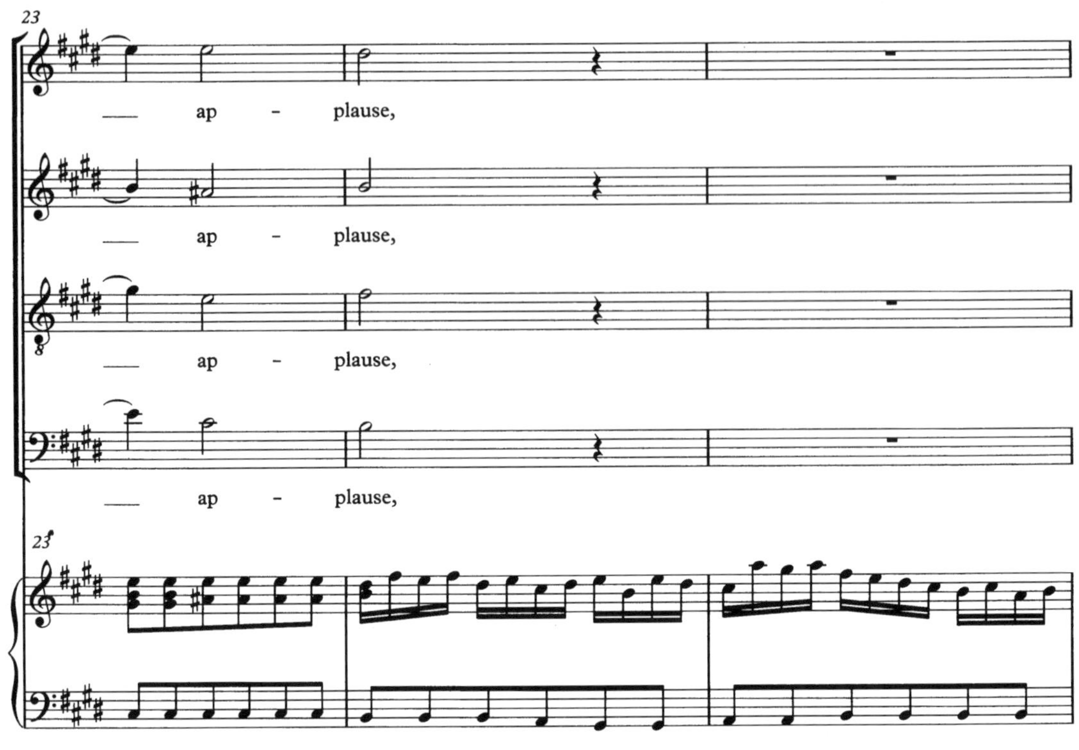

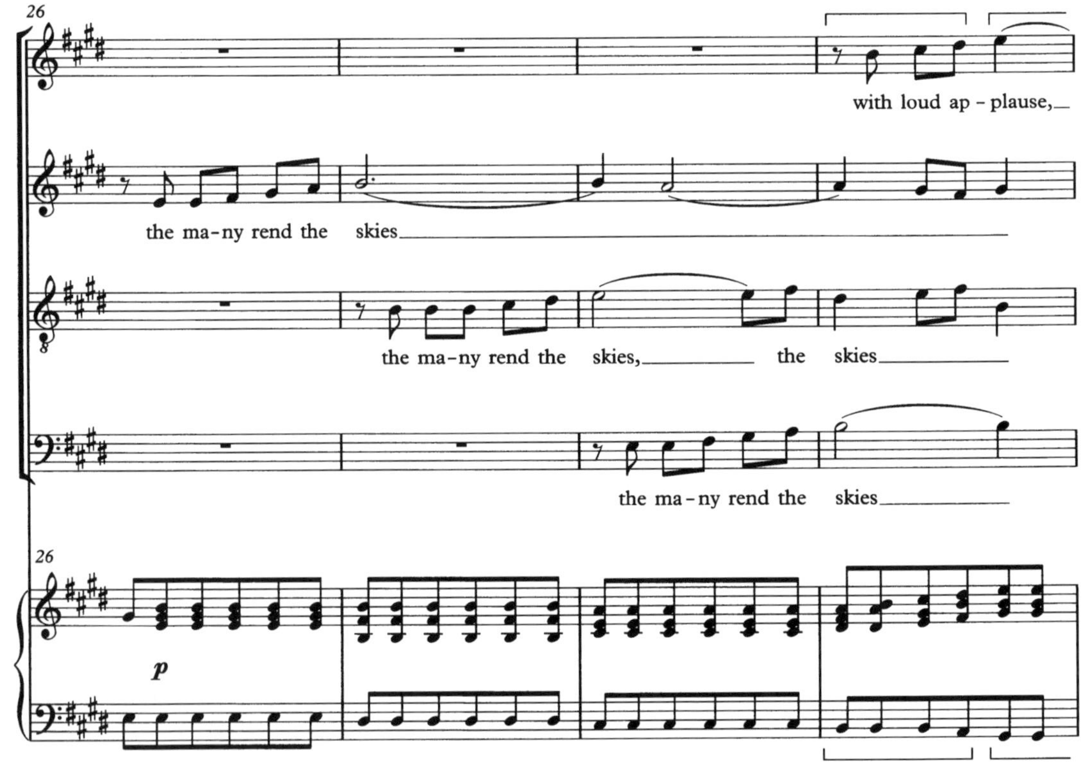

26
with loud ap - plause,
the ma-ny rend the skies
the ma-ny rend the skies, the skies
the ma-ny rend the skies
26
p

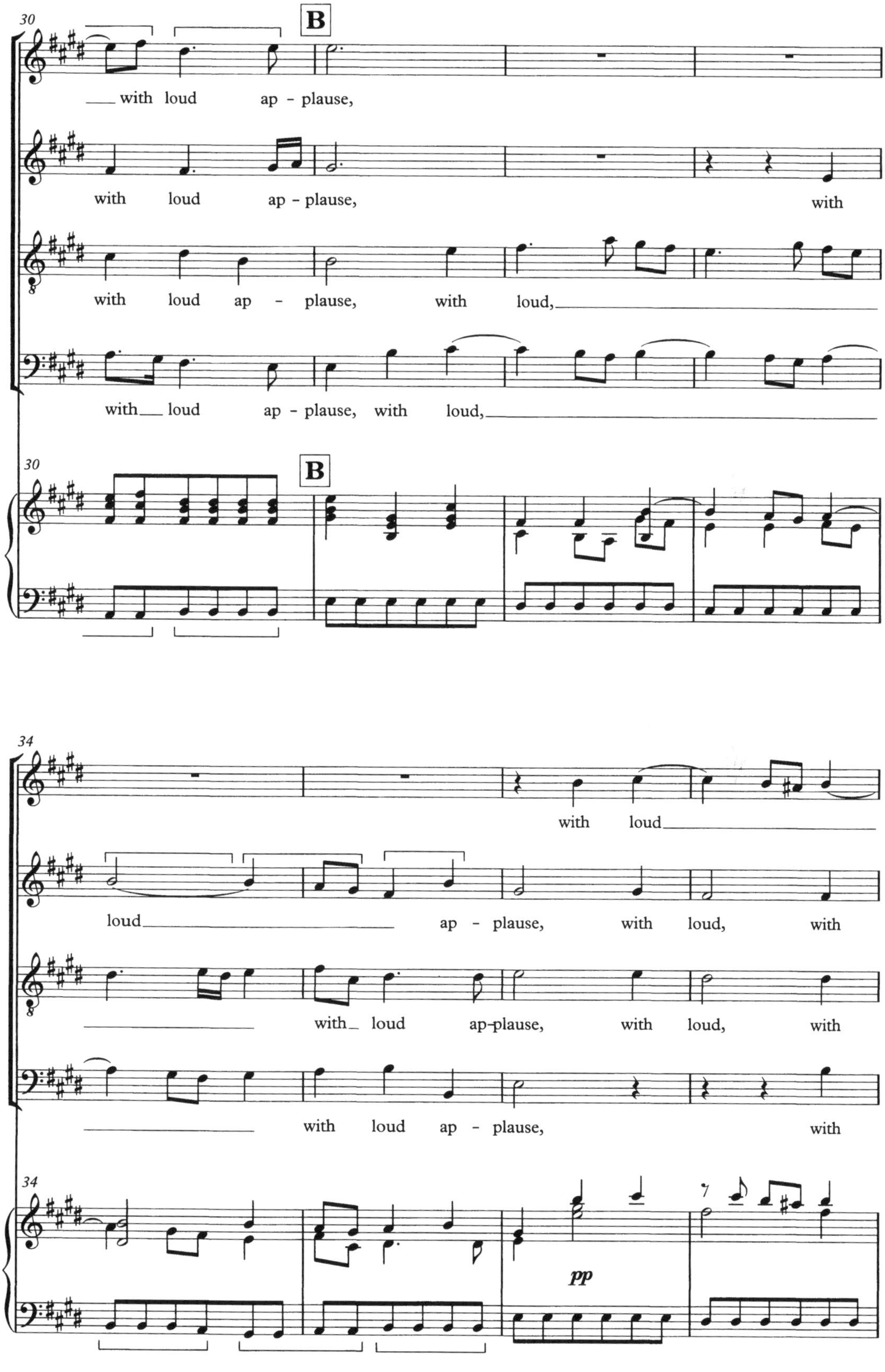

30

B

with loud ap - plause,

with loud ap - plause, with

with loud ap - plause, with loud,

with loud ap - plause, with loud,

30

B

38
ap - plause, with loud
loud ap - plause, with loud
loud ap - plause, with loud
loud ap - plause, with loud
38
f
42
C
ap - plause, the ma-ny rend the skies
ap - plause, the ma-ny rend the
ap - plause,
ap - plause,
42
C
pp

47
with loud ap - plause, with loud ap -
skies,
with loud ap - plause, with loud ap -
the ma - ny rend the skies,
the ma - ny rend the skies,
47
51
- plause,
with loud ap - plause,
- plause,
the ma - ny rend the skies
the ma - ny rend the skies, the skies
the ma - ny rend the skies
51
f

* Bar 60, Soprano. Handel's rhythm ♪♫ adjusted to conform to bar 65.

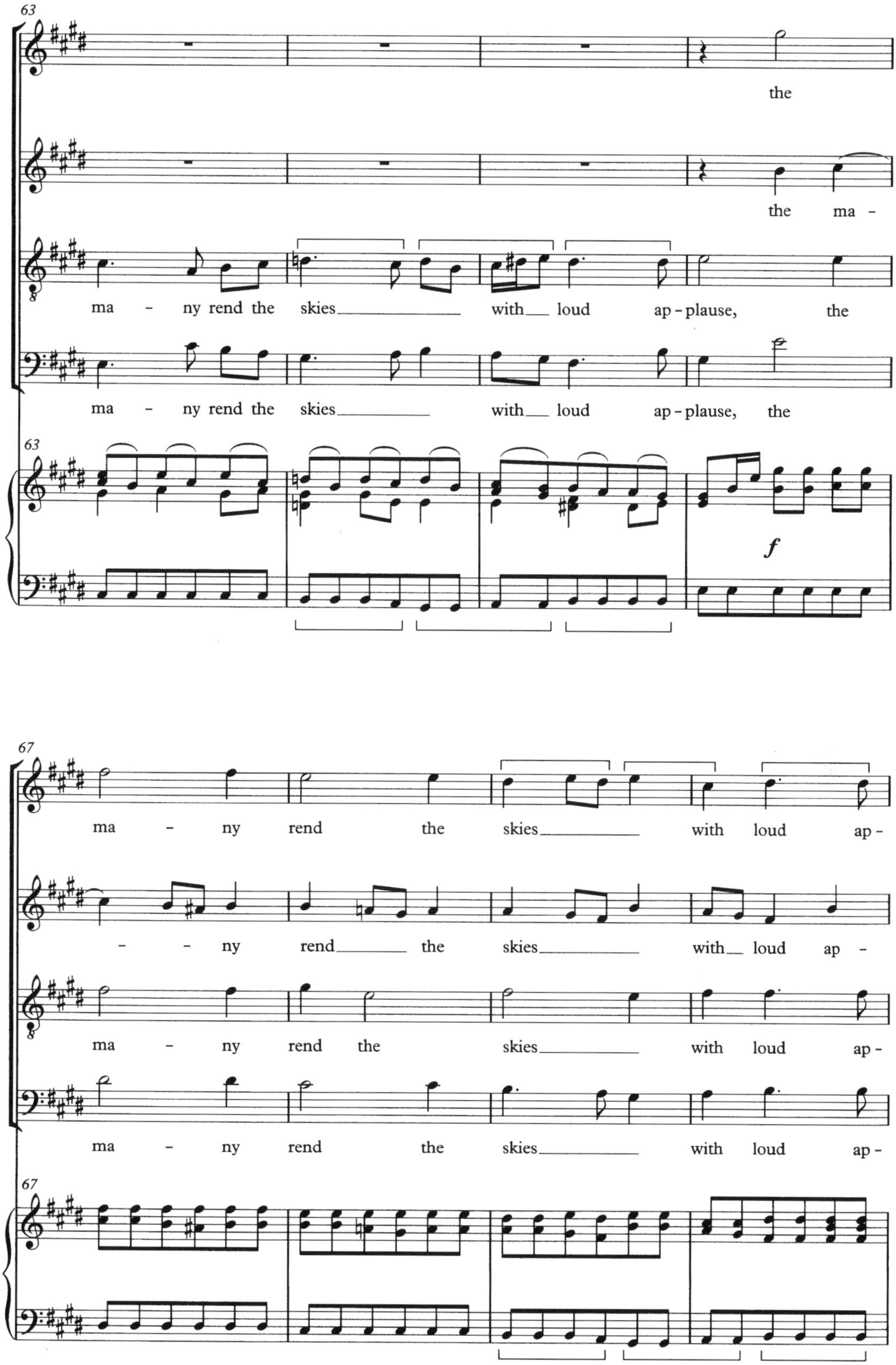

63

the

the ma -

ma - ny rend the skies with loud ap - plause, the

ma - ny rend the skies with loud ap - plause, the

63

f

71
D
Adagio
Allegro
-plause, with loud ap - plause;
-plause, with loud ap - plause;
-plause, with loud ap - plause; so love was
-plause, with loud ap - plause;
71
D
Adagio
Allegro
p
76
so love was crown'd,
but mu-sic won the cause,
crown'd,
but mu-sic won the
76

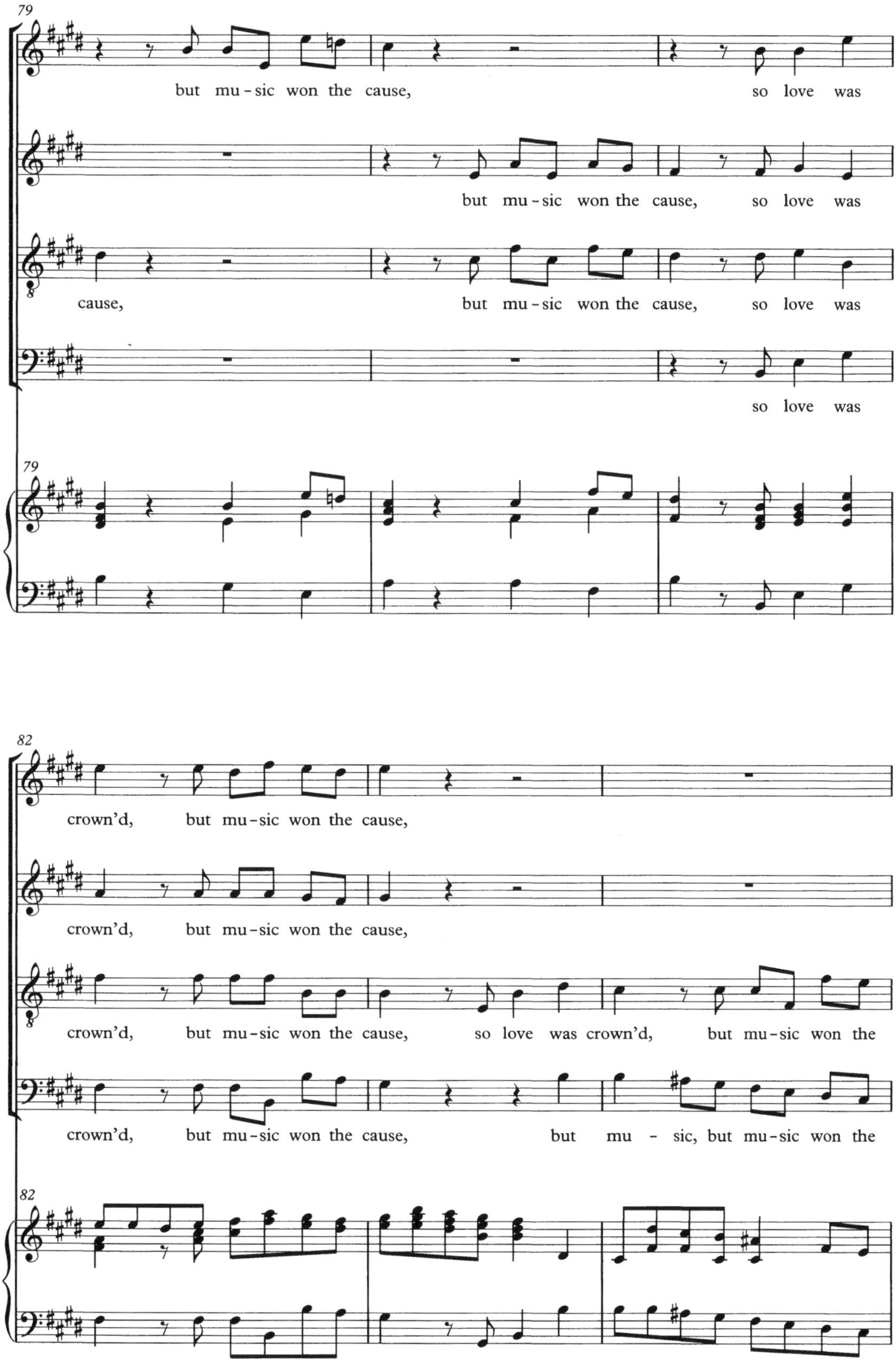

79
but mu-sic won the cause, so love was
but mu-sic won the cause, so love was
cause, but mu-sic won the cause, so love was
so love was
79
82
crown'd, but mu-sic won the cause,
crown'd, but mu-sic won the cause,
crown'd, but mu-sic won the cause, so love was crown'd, but mu-sic won the
crown'd, but mu-sic won the cause, but mu - sic, but mu-sic won the
82

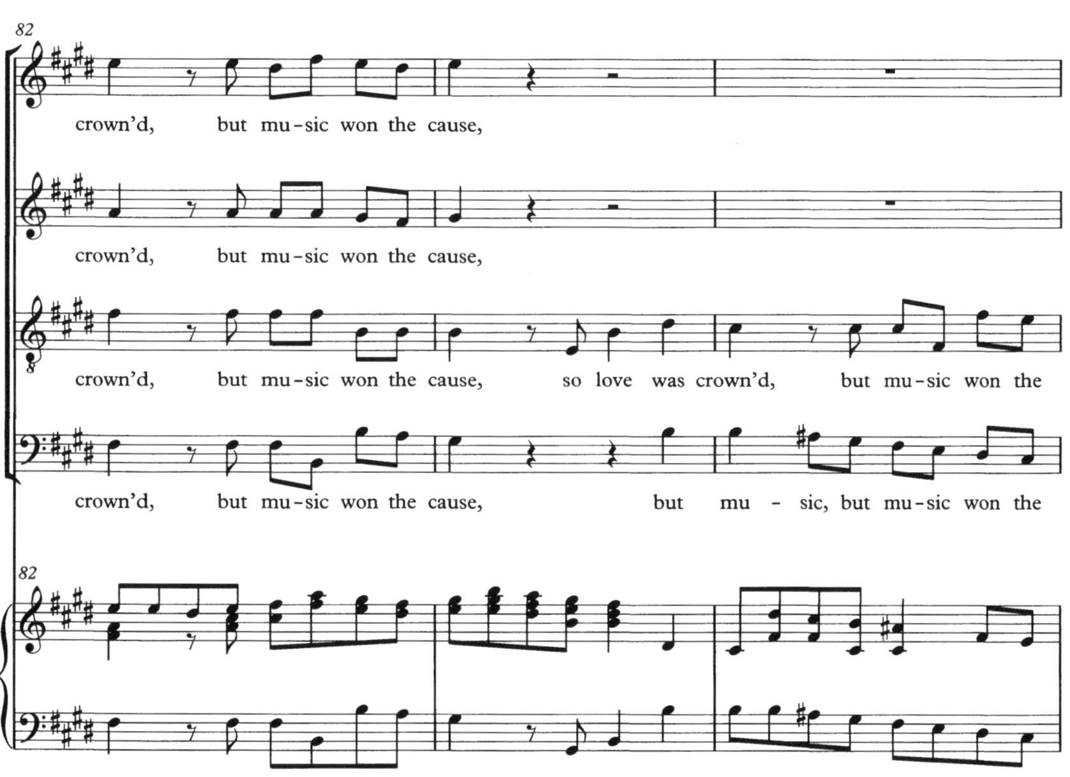

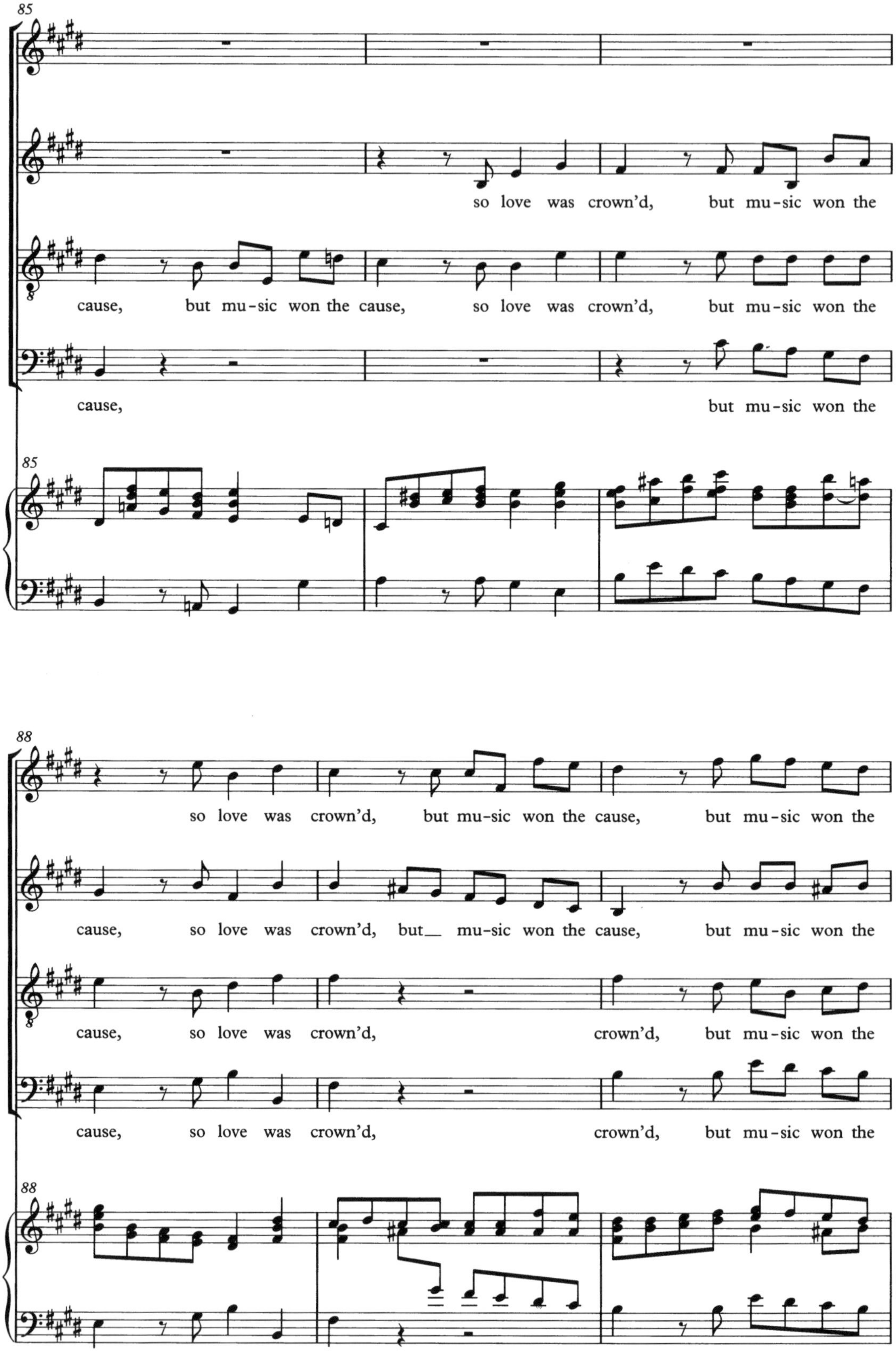

85

so love was crown'd, but mu-sic won the

cause, but mu-sic won the cause, so love was crown'd, but mu-sic won the

cause, but mu-sic won the

85

91 **E**

cause, but mu - sic won the cause, so love was crown'd,

cause, but mu - sic won the cause, so love,

cause, but mu - sic won the cause, so love was crown'd,

cause, but mu - sic won the cause, so love,

91 **E**

94

so love was crown'd, but mu - sic won the cause,

so love was crown'd, so love was

so love was crown'd, was crown'd, but mu - sic won the cause, so love was

so love was crown'd,____ but__ mu - sic won the cause, so love was

94

97
but mu-sic won the cause,
but mu-sic won the
crown'd,
but mu-sic won the
cause,
but mu-sic won the
crown'd,
but_ mu-sic won the
cause,
but mu-sic won the
crown'd,
but mu-sic won the
cause;
97
100
cause;
the ma-ny rend the
cause;
the ma-ny rend the
skies
with
loud_ ap - plause,
cause;
the
ma-ny rend the
skies
with
loud_ ap - plause,
the
100

103
skies with loud_ ap - plause, the ma - ny rend the skies_ with_ loud ap -
the ma - ny rend the skies_ with loud ap -
the ma - ny rend the skies with_ loud ap -
ma - ny rend the skies with loud_ ap - plause, with loud,_ with_ loud ap -
103
106
F
- plause; so love was crown'd, but mu - sic won the cause,
- plause; so love was crown'd, so love was crown'd, but mu - sic won the
- plause; so love was crown'd, so love was crown'd,
- plause; so love was crown'd, so love was crown'd,
106
F

109
but mu - sic won the cause,
but mu - sic won the
cause,
but mu - sic won the cause,
but
crown'd,
crown'd,
crown'd,
but
crown'd,
crown'd,
crown'd,
but
109

112
cause, won the cause,
but mu - sic won the cause,
but mu - sic won the
mu - sic won the cause,
but mu - sic won the cause, won the
mu - sic won the cause, won the cause, won the
mu - sic won the cause, won the cause, won the
112

115
G
cause; the ma-ny rend the skies with loud ap - plause,
cause; the ma-ny rend the skies with loud ap - plause,
cause; the ma-ny rend the skies with loud__ ap - plause,
cause; the ma-ny rend the skies with loud ap - plause, so love was
[più forte]
118
so love was crown'd, but mu-sic won the
so love was
crown'd, but mu-sic won the cause, so love was crown'd,

121
cause,
but mu-sic won the cause,
but
crown'd,
but mu-sic won the cause,
but mu-sic won the
crown'd,
crown'd,
crown'd,
but
124
H
so love was crown'd,
mu - sic won the cause,
so love was crown'd,
but mu-sic won the
cause, won the cause,
so love was crown'd, so love was
mu - sic won the cause,
so love was crown'd,
but mu-sic won the
H

127
so love was crown'd, but mu-sic won the cause, so love was
cause, but mu-sic won the cause, so love was crown'd,
crown'd, but mu-sic won the cause, so love was crown'd, but mu-sic won the
cause, but mu-sic won the cause, but mu-sic won the
127
130
crown'd, so love was crown'd, but mu-sic won the cause, but mu-sic won the
so love was crown'd, but mu-sic won the cause, but mu-sic won the
cause, but mu-sic won the cause, but mu-sic won the cause, but mu-sic won the
cause, but mu-sic won the cause, but mu-sic won the cause, but mu-sic won the
130

133
cause, but mu - sic won the cause, but mu - sic,
cause, but mu - sic won the cause, but mu - sic,
cause, but mu - sic won the cause, but mu - sic,
cause, but mu - sic won the cause, but mu - sic,
133
135
mu - sic won the cause, won the cause.
mu - sic won the cause, won the cause.
mu - sic won the cause, won the cause.
mu - sic won the cause, won the cause.
135

YOUR VOICES TUNE, AND RAISE THEM HIGH

from *Alexander's Feast*

* Bar 5, all voices. 'th'echo' is an abbreviated form of 'they echo'.

6

from the vault - ed sky the blest Ce - ci - lia's name:

from the vault - ed sky the blest Ce - ci - lia's name:

from the vault - ed sky the blest Ce - ci - lia's name:

from the vault - ed sky the blest Ce - ci - lia's name:

6

A

9

mu - sic to heav'n and her we owe, the great - est bless - ing

mu - sic to heav'n and her we owe, the great - est bless - ing

mu - sic to heav'n and her we owe, the great - est bless - ing

mu - sic to heav'n and her we owe, the great - est bless - ing

A

9

12
that's be-low; sound loud - ly then her fame.
that's be-low; sound loud - ly then her fame.
that's be-low; sound loud - ly then her fame.
that's be-low; sound loud - ly then her fame.
B
15
Allegro
20
pp
24
C
Let's i - mi-tate her notes above;
Let's i - mi-tate her notes a-bove;
Let's i - mi-tate her notes a-bove;
Let's i - mi-tate her notes a-bove;
[f]

29

and may this ev'-ning e-ver prove sa-cred to har-mo-

and may this ev'-ning e-ver prove sa-cred to har-mo-

and may this ev'-ning e-ver prove sa-cred to har-mo-

and may this ev'-ning e-ver prove sa-cred to har-mo-

29

33

-ny and love, sa-cred to love, sa-cred to har-mo-ny,

-ny and love, sa-cred to love, sa-cred to har-mo-ny,

-ny and love, sa-cred to love, sa-cred to har-mo-ny,

-ny and love, sa-cred to love, sa-cred to har-mo-ny,

33

37
sa - cred to love,
sa - cred to love,
sa - cred to love,
sa - cred to love,
37

40
sa-cred to love, sa-cred to love, sa-cred to har - mo-ny,
sa-cred to love, sa-cred to love, sa-cred to har - mo-ny,
sa-cred to love, sa-cred to love, sa-cred to har - mo-ny,
sa-cred to love, sa-cred to har - mo-ny,
40

44
D
sa-cred to har - mo - ny and love, sa-cred to love,
sa-cred to har - mo - ny and love, sa-cred to love,
sa-cred to har - mo - ny and love, sa-cred to love,
sa-cred to har - mo - ny and love, sa-cred to love,
44
D
tr
tr
48
sa-cred to love, sa-cred to har - - - - -
sa-cred to love, sa-cred to har - - - - -
sa-cred to love, sa-cred to har - - - - -
sa-cred to love, sa-cred to har - - - - -
48
tr
tr

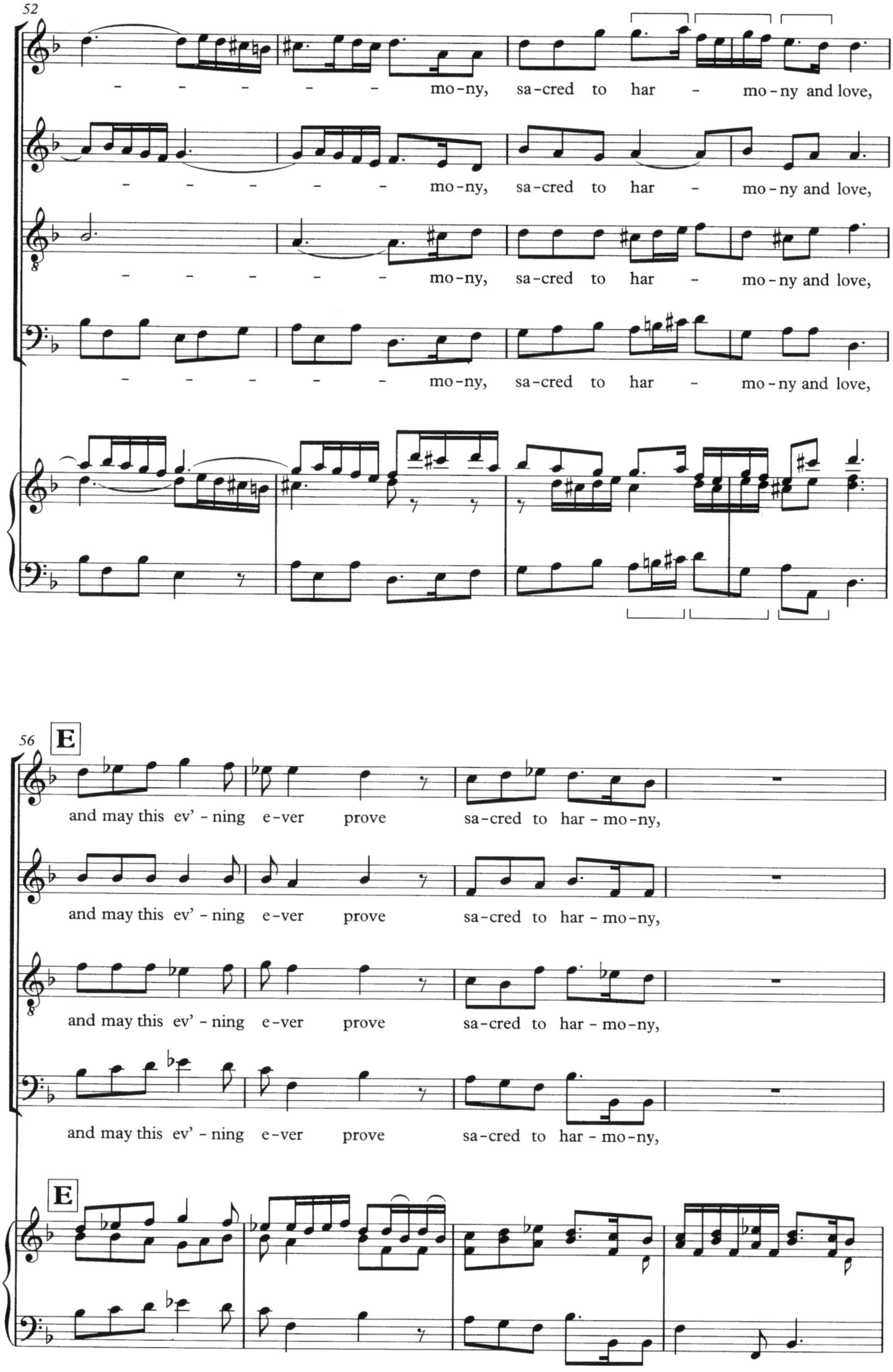

56 **E**

and may this ev' - ning e-ver prove sa-cred to har - mo-ny,

and may this ev' - ning e-ver prove sa-cred to har - mo-ny,

and may this ev' - ning e-ver prove sa-cred to har - mo-ny,

and may this ev' - ning e-ver prove sa-cred to har - mo-ny,

E

64

e - ver prove sa-cred to har-mo-ny, sa-cred to love,

e - ver prove sa-cred to har-mo-ny, sa-cred to love,

e - ver prove sa-cred to har-mo-ny, sa-cred to love,

e - ver prove sa-cred to har-mo-ny, sa-cred to love,

64

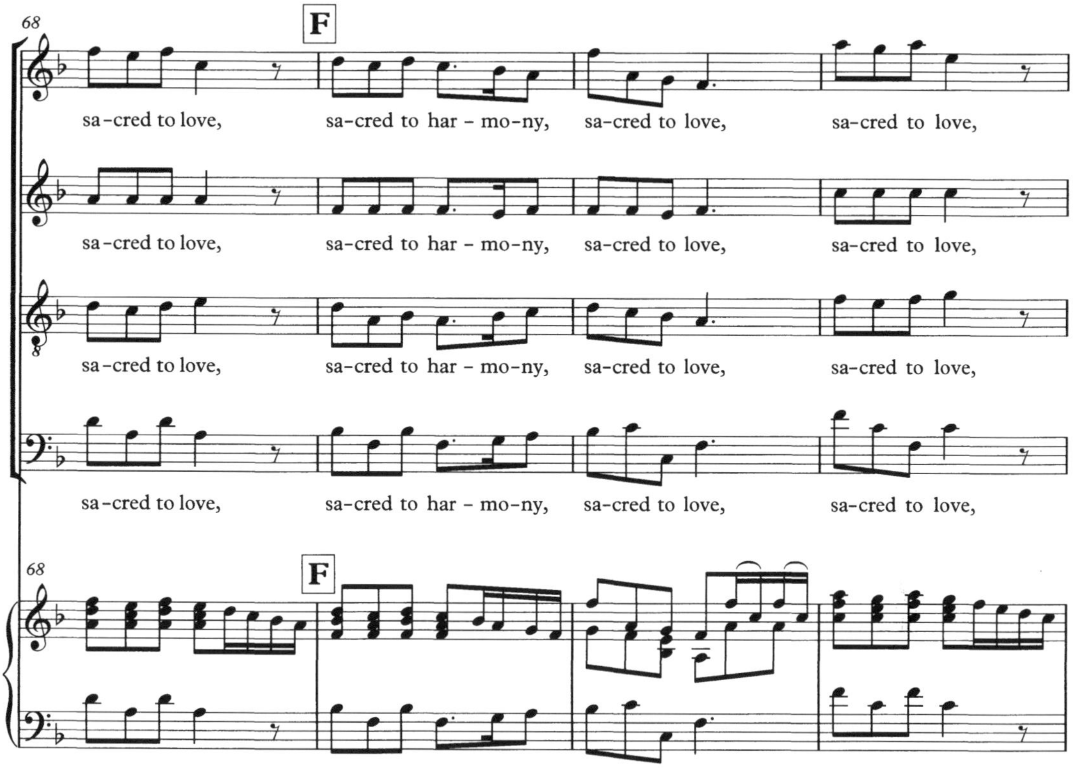

68
F
sa-cred to love, sa-cred to har - mo-ny, sa-cred to love, sa-cred to love,
sa-cred to love, sa-cred to har - mo-ny, sa-cred to love, sa-cred to love,
sa-cred to love, sa-cred to har - mo-ny, sa-cred to love, sa-cred to love,
sa-cred to love, sa-cred to har - mo-ny, sa-cred to love, sa-cred to love,
68
F

72
sa-cred to love, sa-cred to har-mo-ny, sa-cred to love.
sa-cred to love, sa-cred to har-mo-ny, sa-cred to love.
sa-cred to love, sa-cred to har-mo-ny, sa-cred to love.
sa-cred to love, sa-cred to har-mo-ny, sa-cred to love.
72
[tr]

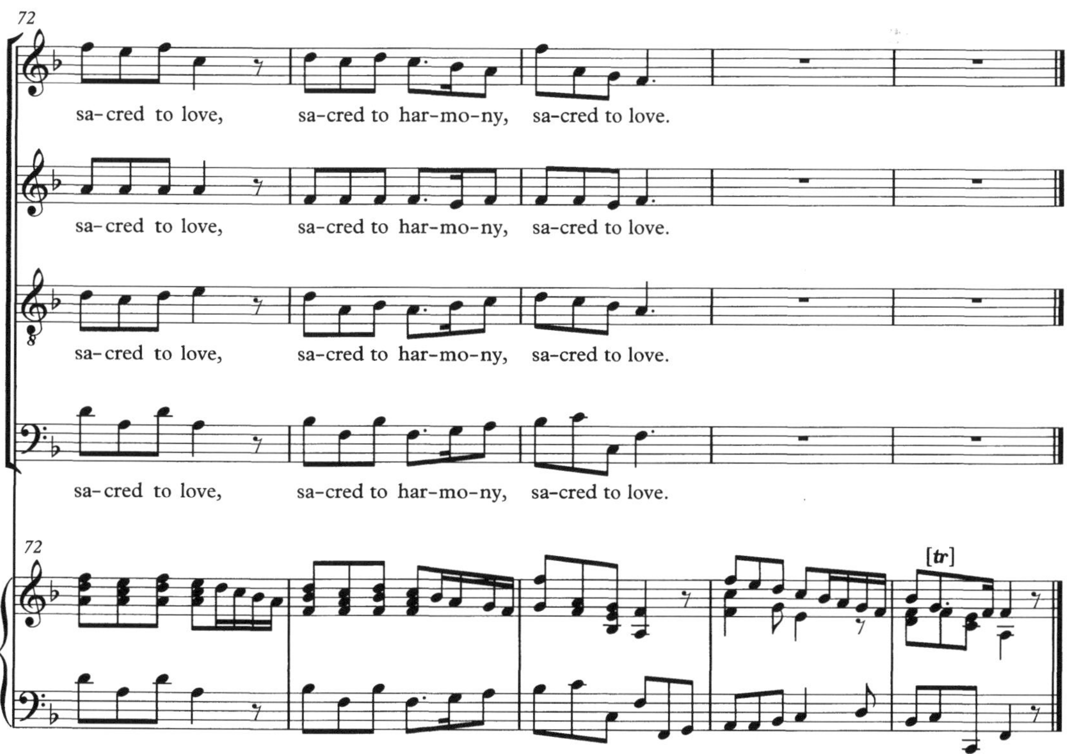

GLORIA PATRI

from *Dixit Dominus*

Psalm cix

13
SOPRANO 2
et Spi-ri-tu-i San-cto, et Spi-ri-tu-i San - cto.
TENOR
Glo - - - - -
13
16
- - ri-a, glo-ri-a Pa - - - - - - - -
19
- - - - - - - - - tri, Pa - tri, et Fi-li-o,
21

24
A
SOPRANO 1
Glo - - - - - - - - - - ri-a, glo-ri-a
SOPRANO 2
Glo - - - - - - - - - - ri-a, glo-ri-a
ALTO
et Spi - ri - tu-i San-cto, et Spi - ri-tu-i San-cto,
TENOR
et Spi - ri - tu-i San-cto, et Spi-ri-tu-i
BASS
Si - - - - - cut e - rat
24
A
27
Pa - - - - - - - - - - - - - - - -
Pa - - - - - - - - - - - - - - - -
et Spi - ri - tu-i San - cto, et Spi - ri - tu-i San - cto,
San - cto, et Spi - ri - tu-i San - cto, et Spi - ri - tu-i
in prin - - - - - -
27

29

- - - - - - - - - - - - - -

- - - - - - - - - - - - - -

et Spi - ri - tu - i San - cto, et Spi - ri - tu - i San - cto,

San - cto, et Spi - ri - tu - i San - - - - cto,

-ci - - - - - pi - o,

29

31

- - - - - tri, glo - ri - a Fi - li - o, et Spi - ri - tu - i

- - - - - tri, glo - ri - a Fi - li - o, et Spi - ri - tu - i

glo - ri - a Pa - tri, et Fi - li - o, et Spi - ri - tu - i San - cto,

glo - ri - a Pa - tri, et Fi - li - o, et Spi - ri - tu - i San - cto,

31

33
San - cto, glo - - - - - - - - - - -
San - cto, glo - - - - - - - - - - -
et Spi - ri - tu - i San - cto, et Spi - ri - tu - i San - cto,
et Spi - ri - tu - i San - cto, et Spi - ri - tu - i
et nunc,
33
35
et Spi - ri - tu - i San - cto, et Spi - ri - tu - i San - -
San - cto, et Spi - ri - tu - i San - cto, et Spi - ri - tu - i
et sem - - - - - -
35

37
B
ri-a,
-ri-a, et Spi-ri-tu-i San-cto, et Spi-ri-tu-i
-cto, glo-ri-a, glop-ri-a Pa
San cto, glo
-per, et Spi-ri-tu-i San-cto,
B
39
et Spi-ri-tu-i San cto,
San-cto, et Spi-ri-tu-i San cto,
tri, si
ria, si
et Spi-ri-tu-i San-cto, et Spi-ri-tu-i San cto,
39

42
et
si - cut e - - - - - - rat
- cut e - - - - - - rat
- cut e - - - - - - rat,
Glo - - - - - - - - - ri - a, glo - ri - a
42
45
Spi - ri - tu - i San - cto,
et Spi - ri - tu - i San - cto,
in
prin - - - - - -
in
prin - - - - - -
et Spi - ri - tu - i
San - cto,
et Spi - ri - tu - i
Pa - - - - - - - - - - - - - -
45

47
et Spi-ri-tu-i San-cto,
et
nunc,
-ci - pio,
et
nunc,
et
-ci - - - pi - o
glo - - - - -
San-cto,
et Spi-ri-tu-i San-cto,
et Spi-ri-tu-i San-cto,
- - tri, et Fi-li - o,
et Spi-ri-tu-i San-cto,
et Spi-ri-tu-i
47
50
et
sem - - - - - -
sem - - - - - - - - - -
et Spi-ri-tu-i San-cto,
et Spi-ri-tu-i San - -
San-cto,
et Spi-ri-tu-i San - - - - - -
50

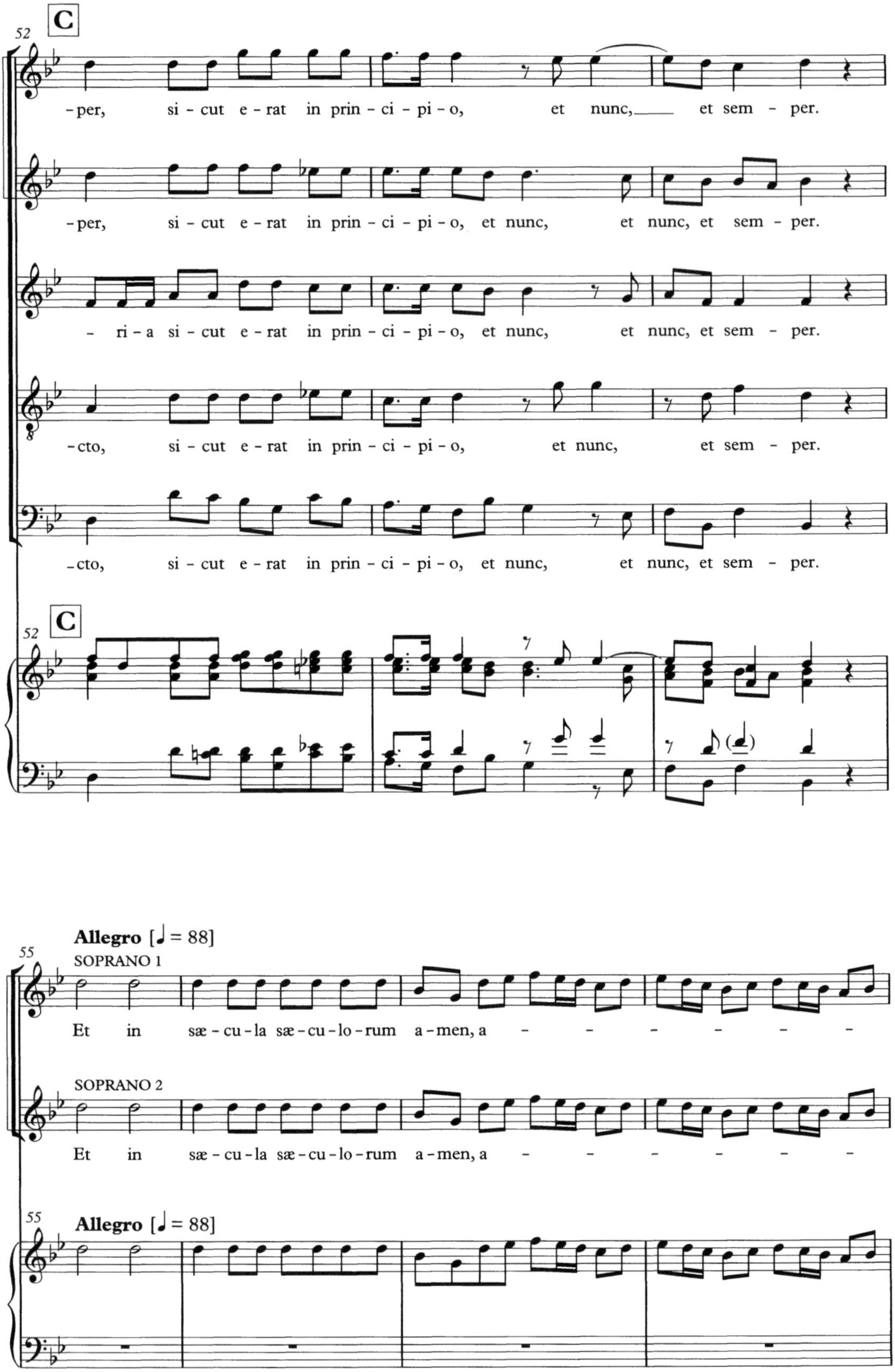

C

52

-per, si - cut e - rat in prin - ci - pi - o, et nunc, et sem - per.

-per, si - cut e - rat in prin - ci - pi - o, et nunc, et nunc, et sem - per.

- ri - a si - cut e - rat in prin - ci - pi - o, et nunc, et nunc, et sem - per.

-cto, si - cut e - rat in prin - ci - pi - o, et nunc, et sem - per.

-cto, si - cut e - rat in prin - ci - pi - o, et nunc, et nunc, et sem - per.

C

52

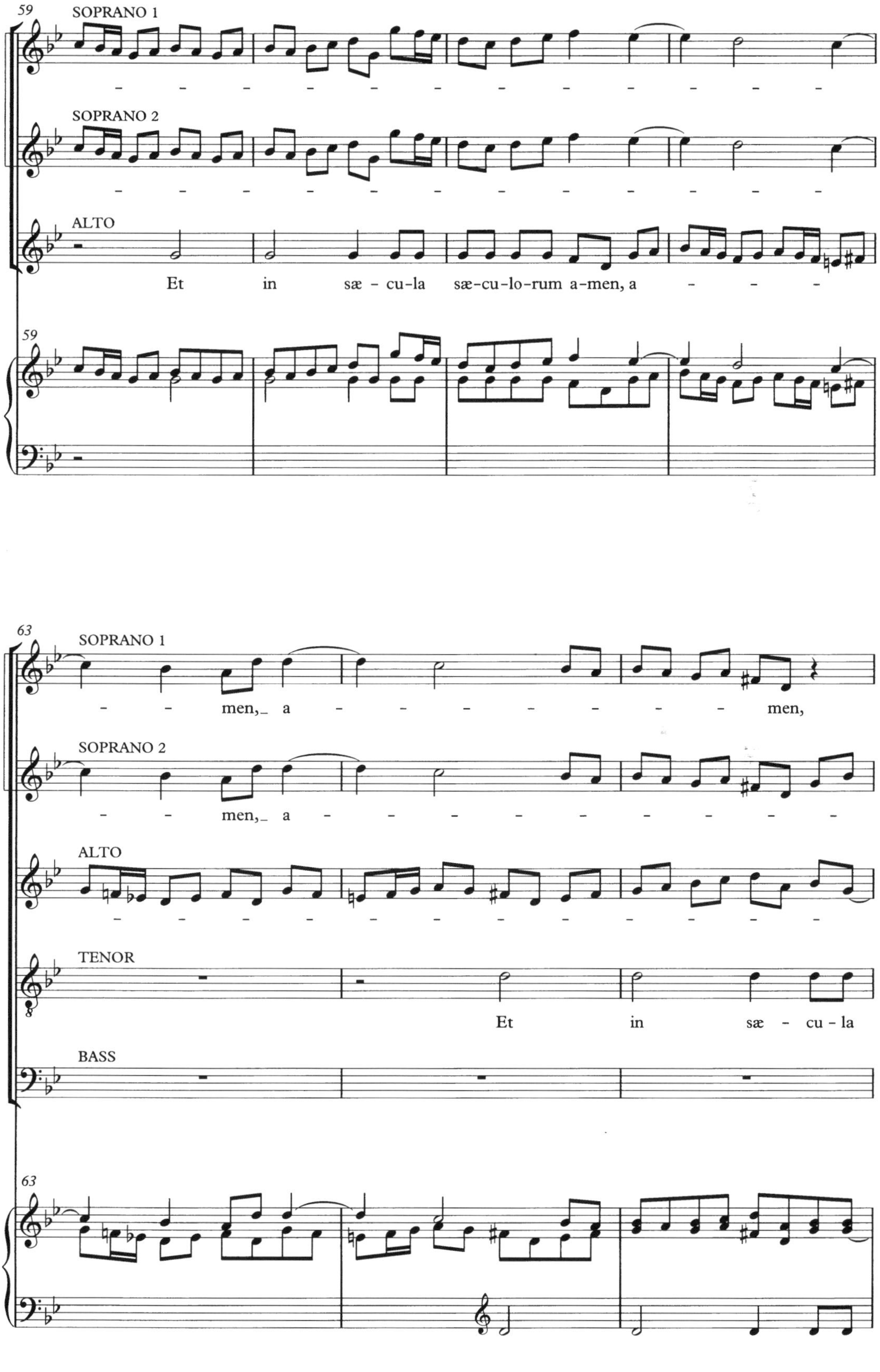

63

SOPRANO 1

men, a - men,

SOPRANO 2

men, a

ALTO

TENOR

Et in sæ - cu - la

BASS

63

66
a
men, a
men,
sæ-cu-lo-rum a-men, a
66
69
men,
men, a
et in sæ - cu-la sæ-cu-lo-rum a-men, a
men, a
et in sæ - cu-la sæ-cu-lo-rum a-men, a
69

72
D
et
men, a
men,
men,
men, a
72
D
75
in sæ - cu - la sæ - cu - lo - rum a - men, a
men, a - men, a
et in sæ - cu - la sæ - cu - lo - rum a
men,
75

78
men,
men,
a
men, a
men,
et
in
sæ - cu - la sæ - cu - lo - rum
et
in
sæ - cu - la sæ - cu - lo - rum
78
81
a
men, a
men,
a-men, a-men,
a-men, a-men,
a - men,
a-men, a
a-men, a
81

84
a – men, a – men, a – men, a – men, a – men, a – men,
a – men, a – men, a – men, a
– men, et
84
87
E
men,
et in sæ – cu – la sæ – cu – lo – rum a –
– men, a – men, a – men, a –
in sæ – cu – la sæ – cu – lo – rum a – men, a – men,
men, a
87
E

90
a
men, a
men,
et in
a
men,
men, a
men,
90
93
men,
et
men, a
sæ cu-la sæ-cu-lo-rum a
a
a
93

96
in sæ - cu - la sæ - cu - lo - rem a - men, a
men,
men,
96
99
men,
men,
a
et in sæ - cu - la sæ - cu - lo - rum
men,
99

102
et in sæ - cu - la sæ - cu - lo - rum a - men, a
a
- men, a - men,
a - men,
a
102
105
- men, a
men, a
a - men,
a
- men, a
105

108
F
men, et in sæ - cu - la
men, et in sæ - cu - la
a - - - - - - men,
- - - - - - men, a - men, et in
- - - - men, a - - men, et in
108
F
112
sæ - cu - lo - rum a - men, a
sæ - cu - lo - rum a - men, a
a
sæ - cu - la sæ - cu - lo - rum a - men, a
sæ - cu - la sæ - cu - lo - rum a - men, a
112

115
115
118
118

121
men, a
men,
men,
a
men, a
men,
a-
men,
121
124
G
a
men, a
men, a
men, a
a
124
G

128

men,

128

131

men, a – men,

– men, a

et in sæ – cu – la sæ – cu – lo – rum a

– men, et in

– men, et in

131

134
a - - - - men, a - - - - - men,
- - - - - - - men, a - -
- - - - - - men, a - - - - - - -
sæ - cu - la sæ - cu - lo - rum a - men,
sæ - cu - la sæ - cu - lo - rum a - men, a - - - - - - - -
134
137
H
a - men, a - men,
- - - - men, a - men, a -
- - - - men, a - men, a -
a - men,
- - - - men, a - men, a -
137
H

140
a – men, a – – – – – – –
-men, a – – – – – – – – – –
-men, a – – men, a – – –
a – – – – – – men, a – men,a –
-men, a – – – – – men, a – – –
140
144
– – – – – – – – – – – – men, et
– – – – – – – – – – – – – – – – – – –
– – – – – – – men, a – –
– men, a – men, a – – – – – men,
– – – – – – – – – – – – men,
144

147
in sæ - cu - la sæ - cu - lo - rum a - - men, et in sæ - cu - la
- - - - - - - - - - men, et in sæ - cu - la
- - - - - - - - - men, et in
a - - - - - - - - - - men, et in
et in sæ - cu - la sæ - cu - lo - rum a - - men, et in
147
151
sæ - cu - lo - rum, et in sæ - cu - la sæ - cu - lo - rum a - -
sæ - cu - lo - rum, et in sæ - cu - la sæ - cu - lo - rum a - -
sæ - cu - la sæ - cu - lo - rum, et in sæ - cu - la sæ - cu - lo - rum
sæ - cu - la sæ - cu - lo - rum, et in sæ - cu - la sæ - cu - lo - rum
sæ - cu - la sæ - cu - lo - rum, et in sæ - cu - la sæ - cu - lo - rum
151

154
J
- men, et in sæ - cu - la sæ - cu - lo - rum a - - - - -
- men, et in sæ - cu - la sæ - cu - lo - rum a - - - - -
a - - men, et in sæ - cu - la sæ - cu - lo - rum a - men, a -
a - - men, et in sæ - cu - la sæ - cu - lo - rum a - men, a -
a - - men, et in sæ - cu - la sæ - cu - lo - rum a - -
154
J
158
- - - - men, a - - -
- - - - men, a - - - - - - - men,
- - - - - - - - men, a - -
- - - - - - - - - - - - - - - men,
- - - - - - - - - - - - - - -
158

165
- - - - - - - men, a - -
a - - - - men, a - -
- - - - - - - - - - - - - - -
- - - - - - - - - - - - - - -
- - - - men, a - - - - - - - -
165

169
men, a
172
men, a
men.
men, a
men.
men, a
men, a
men.
men, a
men, a
men.
men, a
men, a
men.

THE PEOPLE SHALL HEAR

from *Israel in Egypt*

Exodus xv

10

The peo - ple shall hear, and be a - fraid, and be a-

hear, shall hear, and be a - fraid, and be a-

The peo - ple shall hear, and be a - fraid, and be a-

hear,________ and be a - fraid, and be a-

The peo - ple shall hear, and be a - fraid, and be a-

hear, shall hear, and be a - fraid, and be a-

hear, shall hear, and be a - fraid, and be a-

hear, shall hear, and be a - fraid, and be a-

10

13

-fraid, and be a - fraid, a - fraid:

-fraid, and be a - fraid, a - fraid:

-fraid, and be a - fraid, a - fraid:

-fraid, and be a - fraid, a - fraid:

-fraid, and be a - fraid, a - fraid:

-fraid, and be a - fraid, a - fraid:

-fraid, and be a - fraid, a - fraid:

-fraid, and be a - fraid, a - fraid:

13

16
sor - - row shall take hold on
sor - - row, sor - row shall
sor - - row
sor - row shall take hold on
sor - row shall
sor - - row shall take hold,
sor - - row shall take
sor - - row shall take hold on
16
[cresc.]
19
them, shall take hold on them, shall take
take hold, shall take hold, shall take
shall take hold on them, shall take
them, shall take hold, shall take hold, shall take
take hold, shall take hold, shall take
shall take hold, shall take
hold on them, shall take
them, shall take hold, shall take hold on them, shall take
19

22

hold on them. All th'in - ha - bi - tants of

hold on them. All th'in - ha - bi - tants of

hold on them. All th'in - ha - bi - tants of

hold on them. All th'in - ha - bi - tants of

hold on them. All th'in - ha - bi - tants of

hold on them. All th'in - ha - bi - tants of

hold on_ them. All th'in - ha - bi - tants of

hold on them. All th'in - ha - bi - tants of

22

25

Ca - na - an *p* shall melt_ a - way, all th'in-

Ca - na - an *p* shall

Ca - na - an *p* shall melt_ a - way,

Ca - na - an *p* shall

Ca - na - an *p* shall melt_ a - way, all th'in-

Ca - na - an

Ca - na - an *p* shall melt_ a -

Ca - na - an

25

p

28

-ha - bi - tants of Ca - na - an, all th'in - ha - bi - tants of

melt_ a - way, shall melt a - way, all th'in - ha - bi - tants of

shall melt,_ shall melt a - way, all th'in - ha - bi - tants of

melt_ a - way, shall melt_ a - way, all th'in - ha - bi - tants of

-ha - bi - tants of Sa - na - an, all th'in - ha - bi - tants of

shall melt_ a - way, all th'in - ha - bi - tants of

-way, shall melt,_ shall melt a - way, all th'in - ha - bi - tants of

shall melt_ a - way, all th'in - ha - bi - tants of

28

31

Ca - na - an shall melt_ a - way,_ shall

Ca - na - an shall melt_ a - way,_ all th'in - ha - bi - tants of Ca -

Ca - na - an shall

Ca - na - an

Ca - na - an

Ca - na - an

Ca - na - an

Ca - na - an

31

34
melt_ a - way, all th'in - ha - bi - tants of Ca - na - an shall melt a - way,
- na - an shall melt_ a - way,_ shall melt a - way,_
melt_ a - way,_ all th'in - ha - bi - tants of Ca - na - an shall melt a - way,
p
shall
p
shall
34
37
shall melt_ a - way,
shall melt_ a - way,_ shall melt_ a - way,
p
shall melt_ a - way,_ all th'in-
melt_ a - way,_ all th'in - ha - bi - tants of Ca - na - an shall melt_ a - way, shall
p
shall melt_ a - way,_ all th'in-
melt_ a - way,_ all th'in - ha - bi - tants of Ca - na - an shall melt_ a - way,
p
shall melt_ a - way,_ all th'in-
37

40
shall melt a-way, shall melt a-way,_ all th'in-
shall melt_ a-way,_ shall melt a-way,_ all th'in-
all th'in-ha - bi-
-ha-bi-tants of Ca - - - na-an shall melt a-way,___
melt_ a-way,_ shall melt a-way, shall melt a-way,_ all th'in-
-ha-bi-tants of Ca-na-an shall melt_ a-way,_ shall melt a-way, all th'in-
all th'in-ha - bi-
-ha-bi-tants of Ca - - - na-an shall melt a-way,___
40
43
-ha - bi-tants of Ca-na-an shall melt, shall melt___ a-
-ha - bi-tants of Ca-na-an shall melt a-way,___ shall melt a-
-tants_ of Ca-na-an shall melt, shall melt___ a-
shall melt___ a-
-ha - bi-tants of Ca-na-an shall melt, shall melt___ a-
-ha - bi-tants of Ca-na-an shall melt a-way,___ shall melt a-
-tants_ of Ca-na-an shall melt, shall melt___ a-
shall melt___ a-
43

46

- way, shall melt, shall melt a - way, shall

- way, shall melt a - way,

- way, shall melt, shall melt a - way, shall melt a - way, shall

- way, shall melt, shall melt a - way, shall

- way, shall melt, shall melt a - way, shall

- way, shall melt a - way,

- way, shall melt, shall melt a - way, shall melt a - way, shall

- way, shall melt, shall melt a - way, shall

46

49

melt a - way, shall melt a - way, all th'in - ha - bi - tants of

shall melt a - way, all th'in - ha - bi - tants of

melt, shall melt a - way, all th'in - ha - bi - tants of

melt a - way, shall melt a - way, all th'in - ha - bi - tants of

melt a - way, shall melt a - way, all th'in - ha - bi - tants of

shall melt a - way, all th'in - ha - bi - tants of

melt, shall melt a - way, all th'in - ha - bi - tants of

melt a - way, shall melt a - way, all th'in - ha - bi - tants of

49

52

Ca - na - an shall melt_ a - way, shall melt_ a - way,

Ca - na - an shall

Ca - na - an shall melt_ a - way,

Ca - na - an shall melt_ a -

Ca - na - an shall melt_ a - way, shall melt_ a - way,

Ca - na - an shall

Ca - na - an shall melt_ a - way,

Ca - na - an shall melt_ a -

52

55

shall melt a - way, shall melt a - way by the

melt_ a - way,___ shall melt a - way by the

shall melt, shall melt a - way by the

- way, shall melt,___ shall melt a - way by the

shall melt a - way, shall melt a - way by the

melt_ a - way,___ shall melt a - way by the

shall melt, shall melt a - way by the

- way, shall melt,___ shall melt a - way by the

55

58

great – ness of Thy arm, of Thy arm.

great – – ness of Thy arm, of Thy arm.

great – ness of Thy arm, of Thy arm.

great – ness of Thy arm, of Thy arm.

great – – ness of Thy arm, of Thy arm.

great – ness of Thy arm, of Thy arm.

great – ness of Thy arm, of Thy arm.

great – ness of Thy arm, of Thy arm.

61

mp till Thy peo - ple pass_ o - ver, O Lord,

mp till Thy peo - ple pass_ o - ver, O Lord,

mp They shall be as still as a stone

mp till Thy peo - ple pass_

mp They shall be as still as a stone till Thy peo - ple pass_

mp They shall be as still as a stone

mp

65

mp

till Thy peo-ple pass_ o - ver, O Lord, till Thy peo-ple pass_

till Thy peo-ple pass_ o - ver, O Lord,___

till Thy peo-ple pass_ o - ver, O Lord,___

till Thy peo-ple pass_ o - ver, O Lord, till Thy peo-ple pass_

mp

till Thy peo-ple pass_ o - ver, O Lord, till Thy peo-ple pass_

o - ver, O Lord, till Thy peo - ple pass

o - ver, O Lord, till Thy peo-ple pass_

till Thy peo-ple pass_ o - ver, O Lord, till Thy peo-ple pass_

65

cresc.

68

o - ver, which Thou___ hast pur - cha - sed,

which Thou hast pur - cha - sed,

which Thou hast pur - cha - sed; they shall be as still as a stone

o - ver, which Thou hast pur - cha - sed; they shall be as still as a stone___

o - ver, which Thou___ hast pur - cha - sed,

o – ver which Thou hast pur - cha - sed,

o – ver which Thou hast pur - cha - sed; they shall be as still as a stone

o - ver which Thou hast pur - cha - sed; they shall be as still as a stone___

68

72
till Thy peo-ple pass_ o - ver, O Lord, till Thy peo-ple pass_
till Thy peo-ple pass_ o - ver, O Lord,
till Thy peo-ple pass_ o - ver, O Lord,
till Thy peo-ple pass_
till Thy peo-ple pass_ o - ver, O Lord,
till Thy peo-ple pass_ o - ver, O Lord,
till Thy peo-ple pass_ o - ver, O Lord,
till Thy peo-ple pass_
72
75
o - ver, which Thou hast pur - cha - sed,
Thy_ peo - ple_ which Thou hast pur - cha - sed,
which Thou hast pur - cha - sed, till Thy peo-ple pass_
o - - ver which Thou hast pur - cha - sed,_ till Thy peo-ple pass_
Thy_ peo - ple_ which Thou hast pur - cha - sed,
Thy_ peo - ple_ which Thou hast pur - cha - sed,
which Thou hast pur - cha - sed, till Thy peo-ple pass_
o - - ver which Thou hast pur - cha - sed,_ till Thy peo-ple pass_
75

78
till Thy peo-ple pass_ o - ver, O Lord, till Thy peo-ple pass_
till Thy peo-ple pass_ o - ver, O Lord,
o - ver, O Lord,
o - ver, O Lord, they shall be as still as a
till Thy peo-ple pass_ o - ver, O Lord, till Thy peo-ple pass_
till Thy peo-ple pass_ o - ver, O Lord,
o - ver, O Lord,
o - ver, O Lord, they shall be as still as a
78
81
o - - - ver which Thou hast pur - cha-sed,
till Thy peo-ple pass_ o - ver, O Lord,
till Thy peo-ple pass_ o - ver, O Lord,
stone, as a stone,
o - - - ver which Thou hast pur - cha-sed,
till Thy peo-ple pass_
till Thy peo-ple pass_
stone, as a stone,
81

84

till Thy peo-ple pass_ o - ver, O Lord,

till Thy peo-ple pass_ o - ver, O

till Thy peo-ple pass_ o - ver, O

as a stone, till Thy peo-ple pass_

till Thy peo-ple pass_ o - ver, O Lord,

o - ver, O Lord,

o - ver, O Lord,

as a stone, Till Thy peo-ple pass_

84

87

Lord, O Lord,

Lord, O Lord,

o - ver, O Lord, O Lord, till Thy peo-ple pass_ o - ver, O Lord,

till Thy peo-ple pass_

till Thy peo-ple pass_

o - ver, O Lord, O Lord, till Thy peo-ple pass_ o - ver, O Lord,

87

90
till Thy peo-ple pass_ o - ver, O Lord, Thy_ peo - ple_
till Thy peo-ple pass_ o - ver, O Lord, Thy peo - ple
till Thy peo-ple pass_ o - ver
Thy_ peo - ple_
till Thy peo-ple pass_ o - ver, O Lord, Thy peo - ple_
o - ver, O Lord, till Thy peo-ple pass_ o - - ver
o - ver, O Lord, Thy_ peo - ple_
Thy_ peo - ple_
90
93
which Thou hast pur - cha - sed, till Thy peo-ple pass_ o - ver, O
which Thou hast pur - cha - sed, till Thy peo-ple pass_ o - ver, O
which Thou hast pur-cha - sed, till Thy peo-ple pass_
which Thou hast pur - cha - sed, they shall be still, till Thy peo-ple pass_
which Thou hast pur - cha - sed,
which Thou hast pur - cha - sed,
which Thou hast pur-cha - sed,
93
which Thou hast pur - cha - sed, they shall be still, till Thy peo-ple pass_

96

Lord, till Thy peo-ple pass_

Lord, till Thy peo-ple pass_ o - ver, O

o - - ver, O Lord, till Thy peo-ple pass_

o - ver, O Lord,_

till Thy peo-ple pass_ o - ver, O

till Thy peo - ple pass o - ver

till Thy peo - ple pass o - ver

o - ver, O Lord,_

99

o - ver which Thou hast_ pur - cha - sed, till Thy peo-ple pass_

Lord, which Thou hast pur - cha - sed,

o - ver which Thou hast pur - cha - sed,

which Thou hast pur - cha - sed,

Lord, which Thou hast_ pur - cha - sed, till Thy peo-ple pass_

which Thou hast pur - cha - sed,

which Thou hast pur - cha - sed,

which Thou hast pur - cha - sed,

* In the final bars Handel set the words thus: 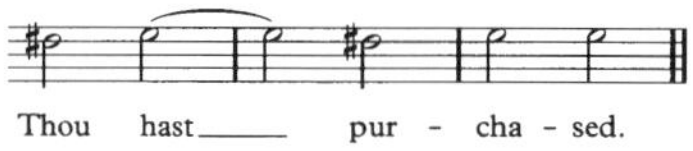

and in the Bass parts: 

SING YE TO THE LORD

from *Israel in Egypt*

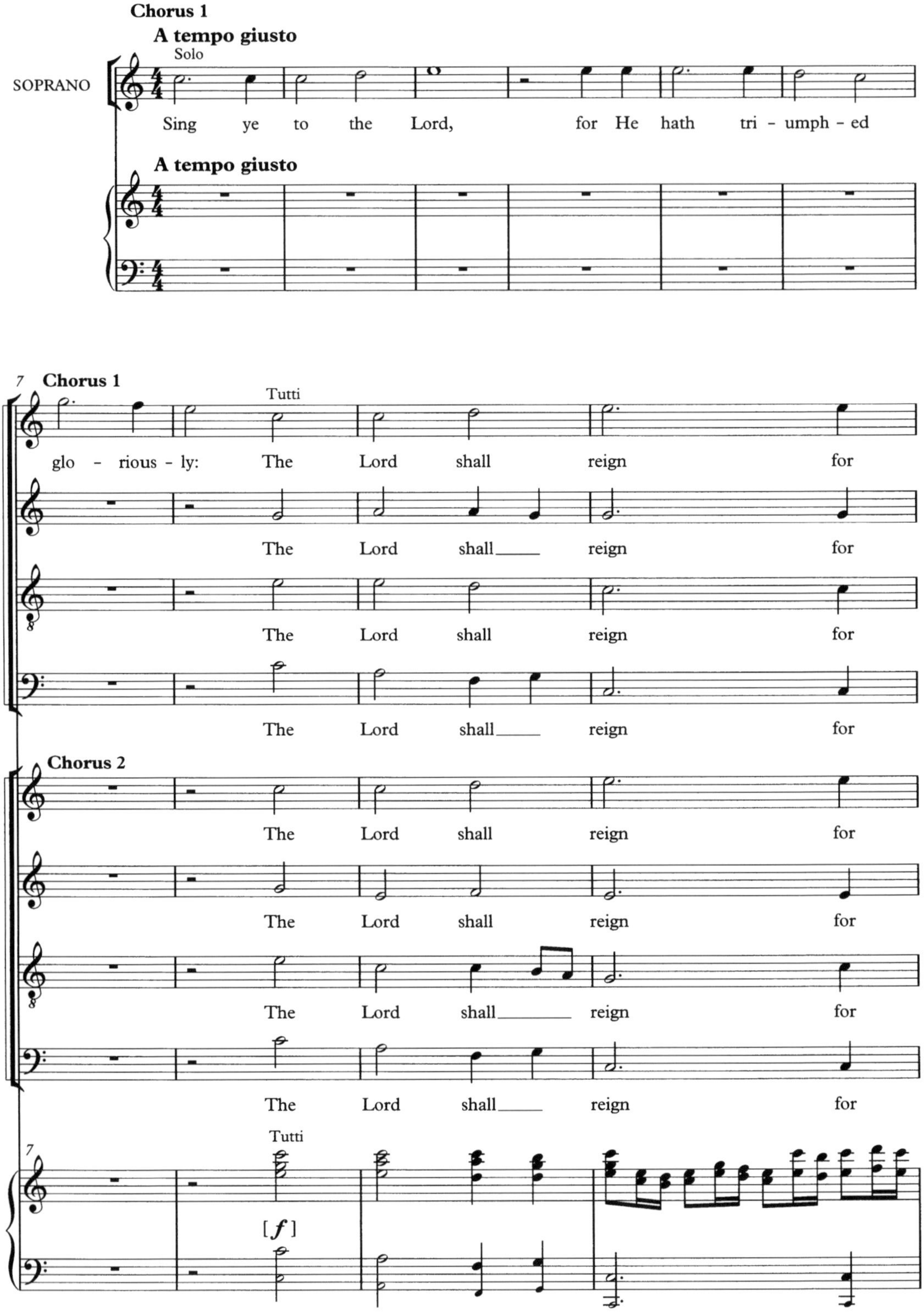

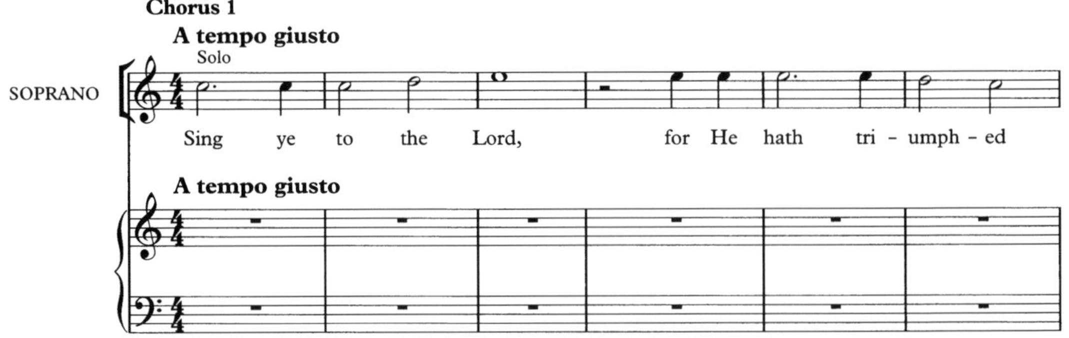

Chorus 1
A tempo giusto
Solo
SOPRANO
Sing ye to the Lord, for He hath tri - umph - ed
A tempo giusto
7
Chorus 1
Tutti
glo - rious - ly: The Lord shall reign for
The Lord shall reign for
The Lord shall reign for
The Lord shall reign for
Chorus 2
The Lord shall reign for
The Lord shall reign for
The Lord shall reign for
The Lord shall reign for
7
Tutti
[f]

11
Solo
e - ver and e - - - - - ver. The
e - ver and e - - - - - ver.
e - ver and e - - - - - ver.
e - ver and e - - - - - ver.
e - ver and e - - - - - ver.
e - ver and e - - - - - ver.
e - ver and e - - - - - ver.
e - ver and e - - - - - ver.
11
14
Tutti
horse and his ri-der hath He thrown in - to the sea. The Lord shall
The Lord shall
The Lord shall
The Lord shall
The Lord shall
The Lord shall
The Lord shall
The Lord shall
14

20

reign for e - ver and e - - - -

reign for e - ver and e - - - -

reign for e - ver and e - - - -

reign for e - ver and e - - - -

reign for e - ver and e - - - -

reign for e - ver and e - - - -

reign for e - ver and e - - - -

reign for e - ver and e - - - -

20

23

-ver, for He

-ver, for He hath tri-umph-ed glo - - - - - - - - - - -

-ver, for He hath tri-umph-ed glo - - - - - -

-ver,

-ver,

-ver, for He hath tri-umph-ed glo - - - - - - - rious-ly,

-ver, for He hath triumph-ed glo - - - - rious-ly,

-ver,

23

26
hath tri-umph-ed glo - - - - - - - rious-ly,
- rious-ly, glo-rious-ly, glo-rious-ly,
- rious-ly, glo-rious-ly, glo-rious-ly, glo-rious-ly,
for He hath tri-umph-ed glo - - - - - rious-ly,
for He hath tri-umph-ed
for He hath tri-umph-ed
for He hath tri-umph-ed
for He
26
29
glo-rious-ly, glo - - rious-ly, glo - - rious-ly, glo -
glo - - rious-ly, glo - - rious-ly, glo - - rious-ly, He
glo-rious-ly, glo-rious-ly, glo-rious-ly, glo-rious-ly, glo-rious-ly, glo-rious-ly, He
hath tri-umph-ed glo - - - - - - - - - - - -
29

32

for He hath tri-umph-ed glo - - - - - - - - -

for He hath tri-umph-ed glo - - - - - -

- - rious-ly,

hath tri-umph-ed glo-rious-ly,

hath tri-umph-ed glo-rious-ly, the

- rious-ly, glo-rious-ly, the

32

35

I will

- rious - ly, I will

- rious - ly, the

the

the horse and his ri - der hath He thrown in - to the sea.

the horse and his ri - der hath He thrown in - to the sea.

horse and his ri - der hath He thrown in - to the sea,

horse and his ri - der hath He thrown in - to the sea,

35

37

sing ______ un - to the

sing, the horse and his ri - der hath He thrown ___ in - to the

horse and his ri - der, the horse and his ri - der hath He thrown ___ in - to the

horse and his ri - der, the horse and his ri - der hath He thrown ___ in - to the

37

39

Lord, ___ un - - to the Lord,

sea, in - to the sea,

sea, in - to the sea,

sea, in - to the sea,

I will

the horse, the

the horse and his ri - der, the

I will

39

41
He
He
sing unto the
horse and his ri-der, the horse and his ri-der hath He thrown in-to the
horse and his ri-der, the horse and his ri-der hath He thrown in-to the
sing un-to the
41
43
hath tri-umph-ed glo
hath tri-umph-ed glo-rious-ly, glo-rious-ly,
He hath tri-umph-ed glo-rious-ly,
He hath tri-umph-ed glo
Lord,
sea,
sea,
Lord,
43

45
- rious - ly,
glo - rious - ly,
glo - rious - ly,
- rious - ly,
He hath tri-umph - ed glo - rious-ly, He
He hath tri-umph - ed glo - - - - - - -
He hath tri-umph - ed glo - - - - - -
He hath tri-umph - ed glo - - -
45
47
the horse and his ri - der
the horse and his ri - der hath He
the horse and his ri - der
the horse and his ri - der hath He
hath tri - umph - ed glo - rious-ly,
- - - - rious-ly.
- - - - rious-ly.
- - - - rious-ly.
47

49

hath He thrown in - to the sea.

thrown in - to the sea,

hath He thrown in - to the sea,

thrown in - to the sea,

the horse and his ri - der, the horse and his ri - der

I will sing

I will sing

the horse and his ri - der, the horse and his ri - der

49

51

I will

the horse and his ri - der, the

the

I will

hath He thrown in - to the sea, in - to the sea,

un - to the Lord, un - to the Lord,

un - to the Lord, un - to the Lord,

hath He thrown in - to the sea, in - to the sea,

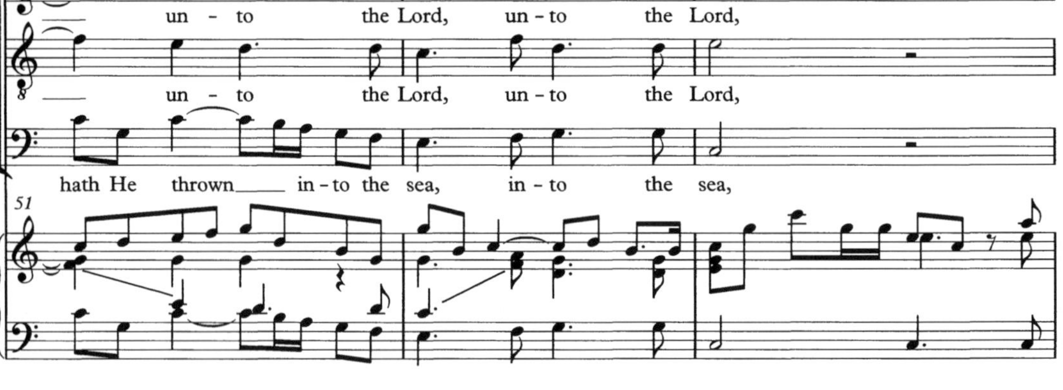

54
Chorus 1
sing unto the
horse and his ri-der, the horse and his ri-der hath He thrown in-to the sea, hath He
horse and his ri-der, the horse and his ri-der hath He thrown in-to the
sing unto the
54
56
Chorus 1
Lord, un-to the Lord, He
thrown in-to the sea,
sea, in-to the sea, He
Lord,
Chorus 2
He hath tri-umph-ed glo-
He hath tri-umph-ed glo-rious-ly, glo-rious-ly,
He hath tri-umph-ed glo-rious-ly, glo-rious-ly,
He hath tri-umph-ed glo-
56

59
hath tri-umph-ed glo - - - - - - - - - - -
He hath tri-umph-ed glo - rious-ly, glo - rious-ly,
hath tri-umph-ed glo - rious-ly, glo - rious-ly,
He hath tri-umph-ed glo - - - - - - -
- rious-ly,
glo - rious-ly,
glo - rious-ly,
- rious-ly,
59

61
- rious-ly, the horse and his ri-der, the horse and his ri-der hath He thrown
glo-rious-ly, the horse and his ri-der, the horse and his ri-der hath He thrown
glo-rious-ly, the horse and his ri-der, the horse and his ri-der hath He thrown
- rious-ly, the horse and his ri-der, the horse and his ri-der hath He thrown
the horse and his ri-der, the horse and his ri-der hath He thrown, hath He
the horse and his ri-der, the horse and his ri-der hath He thrown, hath He
the horse and his ri-der, the horse and his ri-der hath He thrown, hath He
the horse and his ri-der, the horse and his ri-der hath He thrown, hath He
61

64
in - to the sea, the horse and his ri - der, the horse and his ri - der, the
in - to the sea, the horse and his ri - der, the horse and his ri - der, the
in - to the sea, the horse and his ri - der, the horse and his ri - der, the
in - to the sea, the horse and his ri - der, the horse and his ri - der, the
thrown in - to the sea, the horse and his ri - der, the horse and his ri - der, the
thrown in - to the sea, the horse and his ri - der, the horse and his ri - der, the
thrown in - to the sea, the horse and his ri - der, the horse and his ri - der, the
thrown in - to the sea, the horse and his ri - der, the horse and his ri - der, the
64
[ff]

67
Chorus 1 & Chorus 2
horse and his ri - der, the horse and his ri - der hath He thrown in - to the sea, the
horse and his ri - der, the horse and his ri - der hath He thrown in - to the sea, the
horse and his ri - der, the horse and his ri - der hath He thrown in - to the sea, the
horse and his ri - der, the horse and his ri - der hath He thrown in - to the sea, the
67
69
horse and his ri - der, the horse and his ri - der hath He thrown in - to the sea.
horse and his ri - der, the horse and his ri - der hath He thrown in - to the sea.
horse and his ri - der, the horse and his ri - der hath He thrown in - to the sea.
horse and his ri - der, the horse and his ri - der hath He thrown in - to the sea.
69

71
I will sing
I will sing
I will sing unto the
71
74
unto the Lord, for He hath triumphed glo - -
unto the Lord, for He hath triumphed glo - - riously,
I will sing unto the Lord, for He hath triumphed
Lord, for He hath triumphed glo - -
74

77
rious-ly, He hath tri-umph-ed glo - rious-ly, the
glo - rious-ly, glo - rious-ly, He hath tri-umph-ed glo - rious-ly, the
glo - rious - ly, glo - rious-ly, He hath tri-umph-ed glo - rious-ly, the
rious-ly, He hath tri-umph-ed glo - rious-ly, the
77
79
horse and his ri - der hath He thrown in - to the sea, the
horse and his ri - der hath He thrown in - to the sea, the
horse and his ri - der hath He thrown in - to the sea, the
horse and his ri - der hath He thrown_ in - to the sea, the
79

81
horse and his ri - der, the horse and his ri - der hath He thrown in - to the sea, hath
horse and his ri - der, the horse and his ri - der hath He thrown in - to the sea, hath
horse and his ri - der, the horse and his ri - der hath He thrown in - to the sea, hath
horse and his ri - der, the horse and his ri - der hath He thrown in - to the sea, hath
81
83
He thrown in - to the sea.
He thrown in - to the sea.
He thrown in - to the sea.
He thrown in - to the sea.
83

SEE, THE CONQU'RING HERO COMES

from *Judas Maccabaeus*

Thomas Morrell

* The small notes are for rehearsal purposes only.

17
Sports pre - pare, the lau - rel bring, songs of
Sports pre - pare, the lau - rel bring, songs of
Sports pre - pare, the lau - rel bring, songs of
17
Organ
22
tri - umph to him sing. Sports pre - pare, the
tri - umph to him sing. Sports pre - pare, the
tri - umph to him sing. Sports pre - pare, the
22
Hns.
Organ
27
lau - rel bring, songs of tri - umph to him sing.
lau - rel bring, songs of tri - umph to him sing.
lau - rel bring, songs of tri - umph to him sing.
27
[segue]

Chorus of Virgins

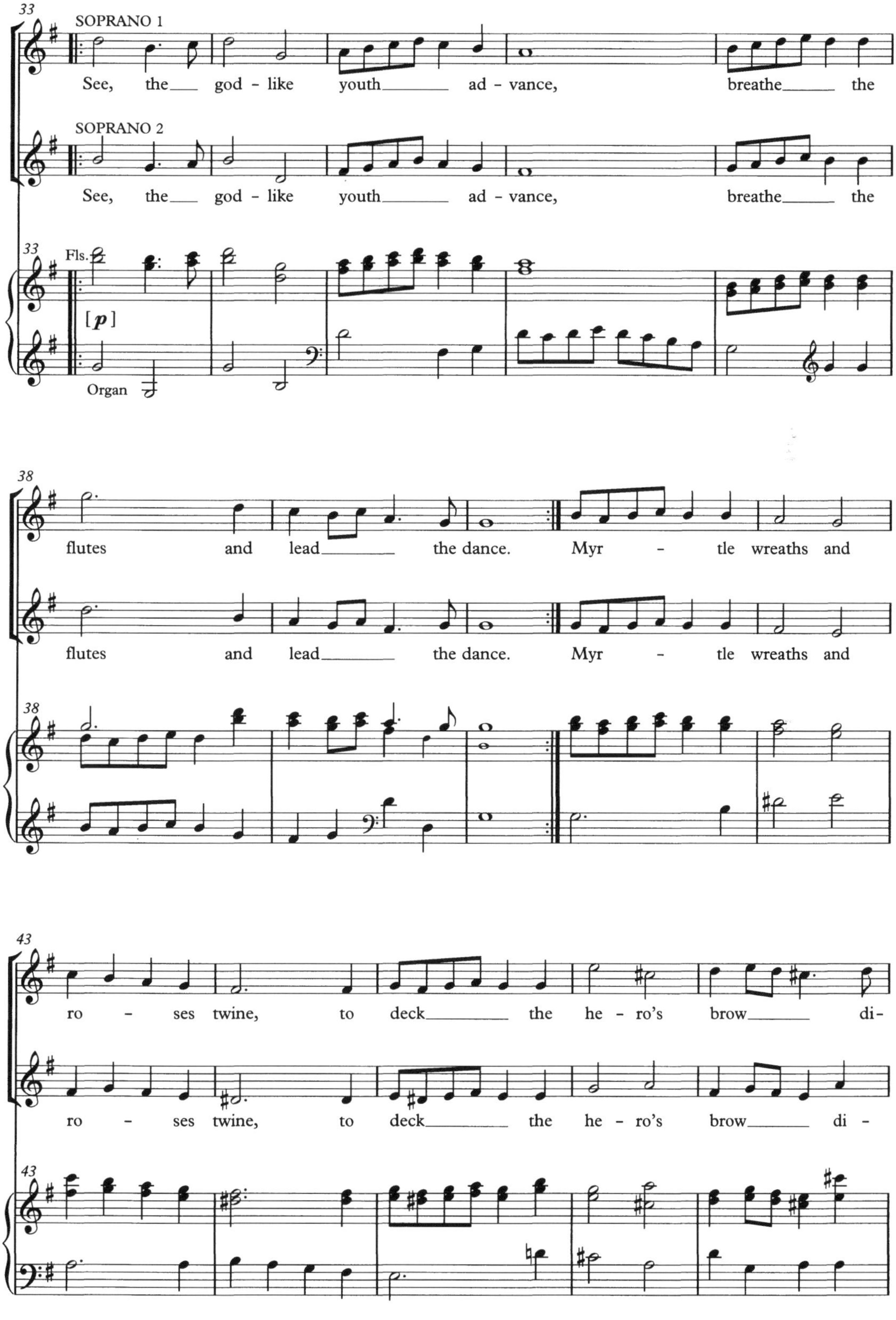

33

SOPRANO 1

See, the god - like youth ad - vance, breathe the

SOPRANO 2

See, the god - like youth ad - vance, breathe the

33 Fls.

[p]

Organ

38

flutes and lead the dance. Myr - tle wreaths and

flutes and lead the dance. Myr - tle wreaths and

38

48

-vine. Myr - tle___ wreaths and ro - ses twine, to___

-vine. Myr - tle___ wreaths and ro - ses twine, to___

48

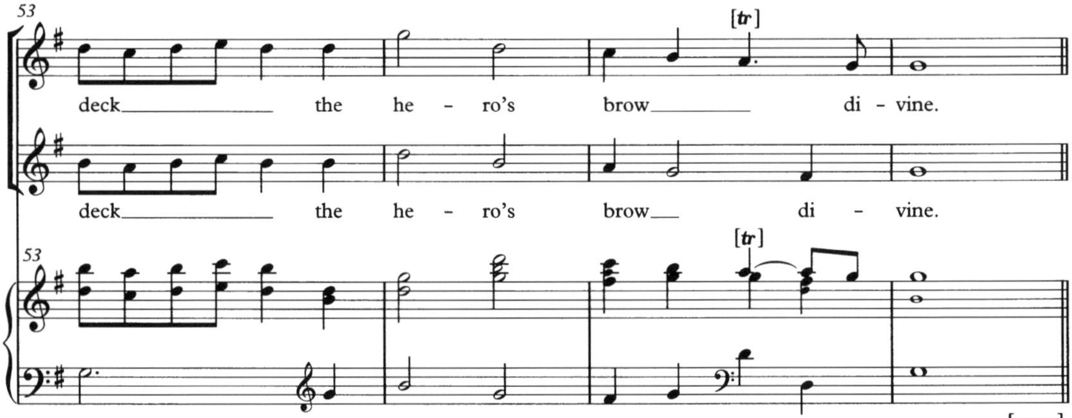

53

[tr]

deck___ the he - ro's brow___ di - vine.

deck___ the he - ro's brow___ di - vine.

53

[tr]

[*segue*]

Chorus of Israelites

* Handel wrote 'Drum ad libitum (i.e. extemporising), the second time warbling (i.e. playing drum rolls).'

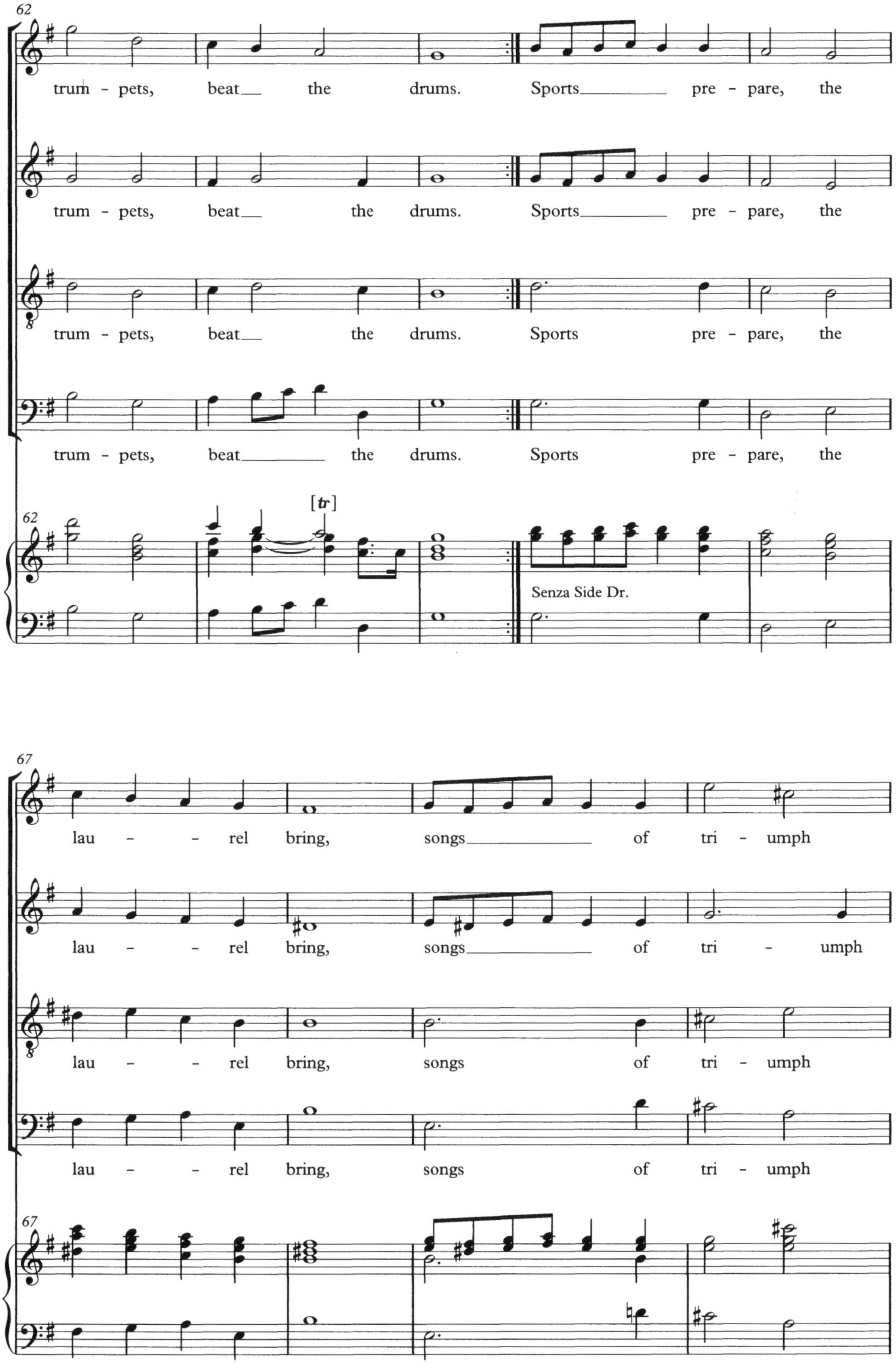

62

trum - pets, beat the drums. Sports pre - pare, the

trum - pets, beat the drums. Sports pre - pare, the

trum - pets, beat the drums. Sports pre - pare, the

trum - pets, beat the drums. Sports pre - pare, the

62 [tr]

Senza Side Dr.

71

to him sing. See, the con - qu'ring he - - ro

to him sing. See, the con - qu'ring he - - ro

to him sing. See, the con - qu'ring he - - ro

to him sing. See, the con - qu'ring he - - ro

71

+ Side Dr.

76

comes, sound the trum - pets, beat the drums.

comes, sound the trum - pets, beat the drums.

comes, sound the trum - pets, beat the drums.

comes, sound the trum - pets, beat the drums.

76

[tr]

March

SING UNTO GOD

from *Judas Maccabaeus*

16
high af - fec - tions raise, to crown this con - quest with un - mea - sur'd praise,
19
[tr]
with un - mea - sur'd praise.
Chorus
SOPRANO
22
[f]
Sing un - to God, and high af - fec - tions raise, to crown this con - quest with
ALTO
[f]
Sing un - to God, and high af - fec - tions raise, to crown this con - quest with
TENOR
[f]
Sing un - to God, and high af - fec - tions raise, to crown this con - quest with
BASS
[f]
Sing un - to God, and high af - fec - tions raise, to crown this con - quest with
22
[f]

25
un-mea-sur'd praise, with un - mea - sur'd, with un-mea - sur'd praise.
un-mea - sur'd praise, with un - mea - sur'd, with un-mea - sur'd praise,
un-mea - sur'd praise, with un - mea - sur'd, with un-mea - sur'd praise, with
un-mea - sur'd praise, with
25

28
Sing un - to God, and
to crown,
un-mea - sur'd praise, to crown, to
un-mea - sur'd praise, with un - mea-sur'd praise,
28

31
high af-fec-tions raise, to crown this con-quest with un-mea - sur'd praise,
to crown, to crown this con- quest, to crown this con-quest with
crown this con-quest, to crown this con-quest, this
31

34
with un- mea - sur'd praise.
un- mea - sur'd praise, to crown this con-quest with un - mea - sur'd praise.
con-quest, to crown this con-quest with un mea-sur'd praise.
O sing.
34

40

high af - fec - tions raise, to crown, to crown,

God, and high af - fec - tions raise,

sing un - to God, and high af - fec - tions raise, to crown this con - quest to

high af - fec - tions raise, to crown this con - quest, to

40

43
to crown, to crown this con-quest,
to crown this con-quest, to crown, to
crown this con-quest, to crown, to crown,
crown this con-quest with un-mea - sur'd praise, to crown
43

46
with un-mea - sur'd praise,
crown this con-quest with un - mea - sur'd praise, to crown, to crown, to crown
to crown this con-quest with un-mea-sur'd praise, to crown,
this con-quest with un-mea-sur'd, with un-mea-sur'd praise, to crown, to crown, to
46

49
to crown this con-quest, this con-quest with un-mea-sur'd praise.
this con-quest, this con-quest with un-mea-sur'd praise.
to crown this con-quest, this con-quest with un-mea-sur'd praise.
crown, to crown this con-quest, this con-quest with un-mea-sur'd praise.
49
52
[ff]
Sing un-to God, sing un-to God, and high af-fec-tions raise, and
[ff]
Sing un-to God, sing un-to God, and high af-fec-tions raise, and
[ff]
Sing un-to God, sing un-to God, and high af-fec-tions raise, and
[ff]
Sing un-to God, sing un-to God, and high af-fec-tions raise, and
52
[ff]

55
high af - fec - tions raise, to crown, to crown, to crown, to crown this con-quest
high af - fec - tions_ raise, to crown, to crown, to crown this con-quest with
high af - fec - tions_ raise, to crown, to crown, to_ crown, to crown this con-quest
high af - fec-tions, raise, to crown, to crown, to crown this con-quest with
55
58
with un - mea - sur'd praise,
un - mea - sur'd_ praise,
with un - mea - sur'd praise,
un - mea - sur'd praise,
58

60
to crown
to crown
with un-mea-sur'd praise, to crown
with un-mea-sur'd praise, to crown
60

63
this con-quest with un - mea - sur'd praise.
this con-quest with un - mea - sur'd praise.
this con-quest with un - mea - sur'd praise.
this con-quest with un - mea - sur'd praise.
63

REJOICE, O JUDAH. HALLELUJAH, AMEN

from *Judas Maccabaeus*

16
[tr]
songs di-vine, with Che-ru-bin and Se-ra-phin, har-mo-nious join. Re-
19
-joice, O Ju-dah, re-joice, re-joice, O
[sim.]
p
22
Ju-dah, re-joice, and in songs di-vine, with Che-ru-bin and Se-ra-phin, har-
25
-mo-nious join, and in songs di-vine, har-mo-nious join. Re-

28
-joice, O Ju-dah, re-joice, O Ju-dah, re-
f
p
31
-joice, re- joice, with Che-ru-bin and Se-ra-phin,
34
har-mo-nious join in
37
[tr]
songs di-vine, with Che-ru-bin and Se-ra-phin, har-
[sim.]

40
[tr]
-mo - nious, har-mo - nious join.
[f]
43
[sim.]
46
BASS SOLO [f]
Hal - le - lu - jah, A-men, A-men, Hal - le - lu - jah, A -
[f]
49
SOPRANO Chorus
[f]
Hal - le - lu - jah, A - men,
ALTO Chorus
[f]
Hal - le - lu - jah, A - men, A - men, Hal - le - lu - jah, A - men, Hal - le - lu - jah,
TENOR Chorus
[f]
Hal - le - lu - jah, A - men, A - men, Hal - le - lu - jah, A - men, Hal - le - lu - jah, Hal - le-
BASS Chorus
[f]
-men,
Hal - le - lu - jah, A - men,
49
tr

52
A - men, Hal - le - lu - jah, A - men, A - men, A - men, Hal -
Hal - le - lu - jah, Hal - le - lu - jah, Hal - le - lu - jah, Hal -
- lu - jah, Hal - le lu - jah, Hal - le - lu - jah, Hal -
A - men, Hal - le - lu - jah, Hal - le - lu - jah, Hal -
52

55
- le - lu - jah, Hal - le - lu - jah, Hal - le - lu -
- le - lu - jah, Hal - le - lu - jah, A - men, A - men, Hal - le - lu - jah, A -
- le - lu - jah, Hal - le - lu - jah,
- le - lu - jah, Hal - le - lu - jah, A - men, A - men, Hal - le - lu - jah, A -
55

58

-jah, Hal - le - lu - jah, A - men, A - men, Hal - le - lu - jah, A - men, O Ju - dah, re-

-men. O Ju - dah, re-

Hal - le - lu - jah, A - men, A - men, Hal - le - lu - jah, A - men. O Ju - dah, re-

-men, O Ju - dah, re-

58

61

-joice, re - joice,____ re - joice,___ O_ Ju-dah, in songs di -

-joice, re - joice,____ re - joice, O Ju-dah, in songs di -

-joice, re - joice,____ re - joice,___ O_ Ju-dah, in songs di -

-joice, re - joice,____ re - joice,___ O_ Ju-dah, in songs di -

61

[*sim.*]

64
-vine, with Che-ru-bin and Se-ra-phin, har-mo - nious join, with Che-ru-bin and
-vine, with Che-ru-bin and Se-ra-phin, har-mo - nious join, with Che-ru-bin and
-vine, with Che-ru-bin and Se-ra-phin, har-mo - nious join, with Che-ru-bin and
-vine, with Che-ru-bin and
64

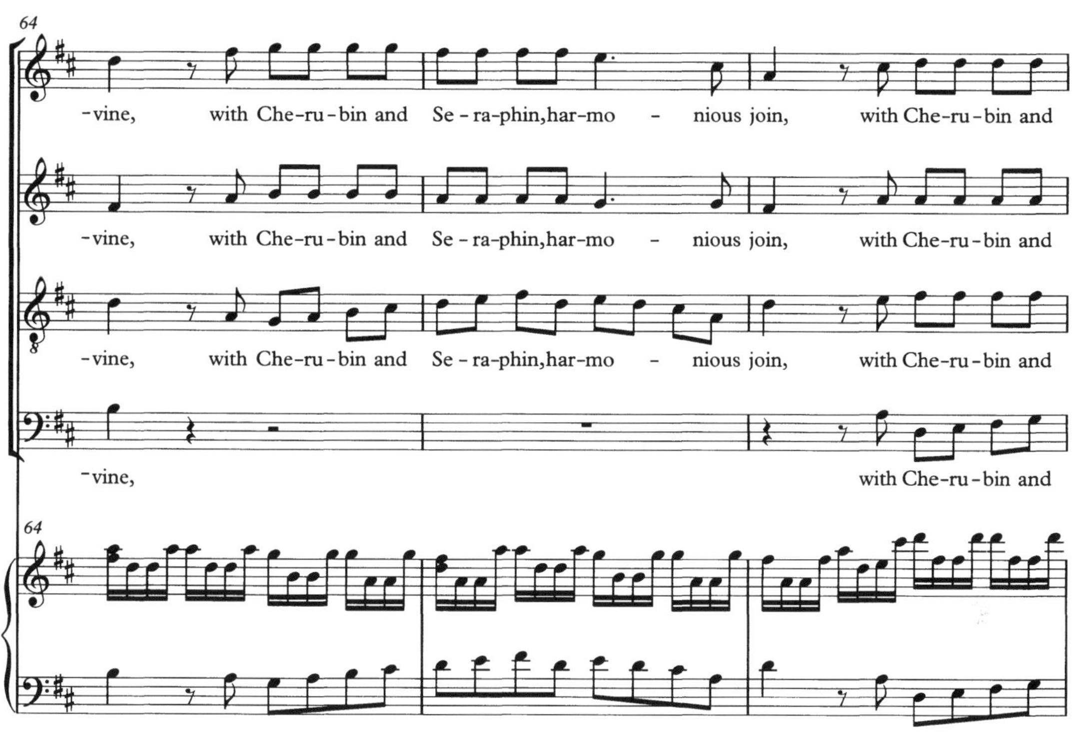

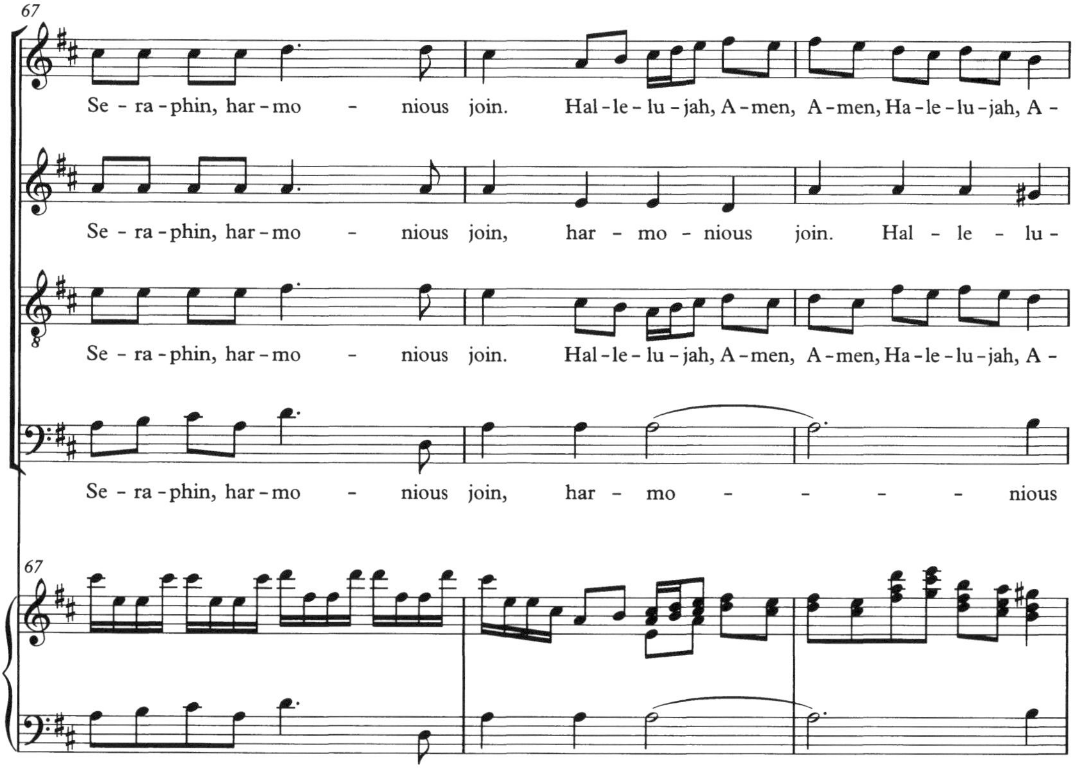

67
Se - ra - phin, har - mo - nious join. Hal - le - lu - jah, A - men, A - men, Ha - le - lu - jah, A -
Se - ra - phin, har - mo - nious join, har - mo - nious join. Hal - le - lu -
Se - ra - phin, har - mo - nious join. Hal - le - lu - jah, A - men, A - men, Ha - le - lu - jah, A -
Se - ra - phin, har - mo - nious join, har - mo - - - - nious
67

70
-men, and in songs di - vine, har -
-jah, and in songs di - vine, har -
-men, and in songs di - vine, har -
join, and in songs di - vine, har -
70
[sim.]

73
-mo - nious join. Hal - le - lu - jah, A - men, A - men, Hal - le - lu - jah, A -
-mo - - nious join. Ha - le - lu - jah, A - men, A - men, Hal - le - lu - jah, A -
-mo - - nious join. Hal - le - lu - jah, A - men, A - men, Hal - le - lu - jah, A -
-mo - - nious join. Hal - le - lu - jah, A - men, A - men, Hal - le - lu - jah, A -
73

76

-men, A - men,

-men, A - men,

-men, A - men,

-men, A - men,

76

FOR UNTO US A CHILD IS BORN

from *Messiah*

Isaiah ix, 6

13
for un-to us a child is born:
us a child is born, un-to us a son is
13
16
B
[p]
For un-to
gi-ven, un-to us a son is gi-ven:
16
B

[p]
us a child is born,
un - to us
a son is
For un-to us a child is born,

gi - ven,
un - to us
a son is gi-ven,
un-to
un-to us

25
C
us a son is gi - ven:
[mf]
and the go - vern - ment shall be up - on his shoul -
a son is gi - ven:
25
C

28
[mf]
and the go - vern - ment shall be up - on his shoul - - - - - -
[mf]
and the go - vern - ment shall
- - - - der:
[mf]
and the go - vern - ment shall
28

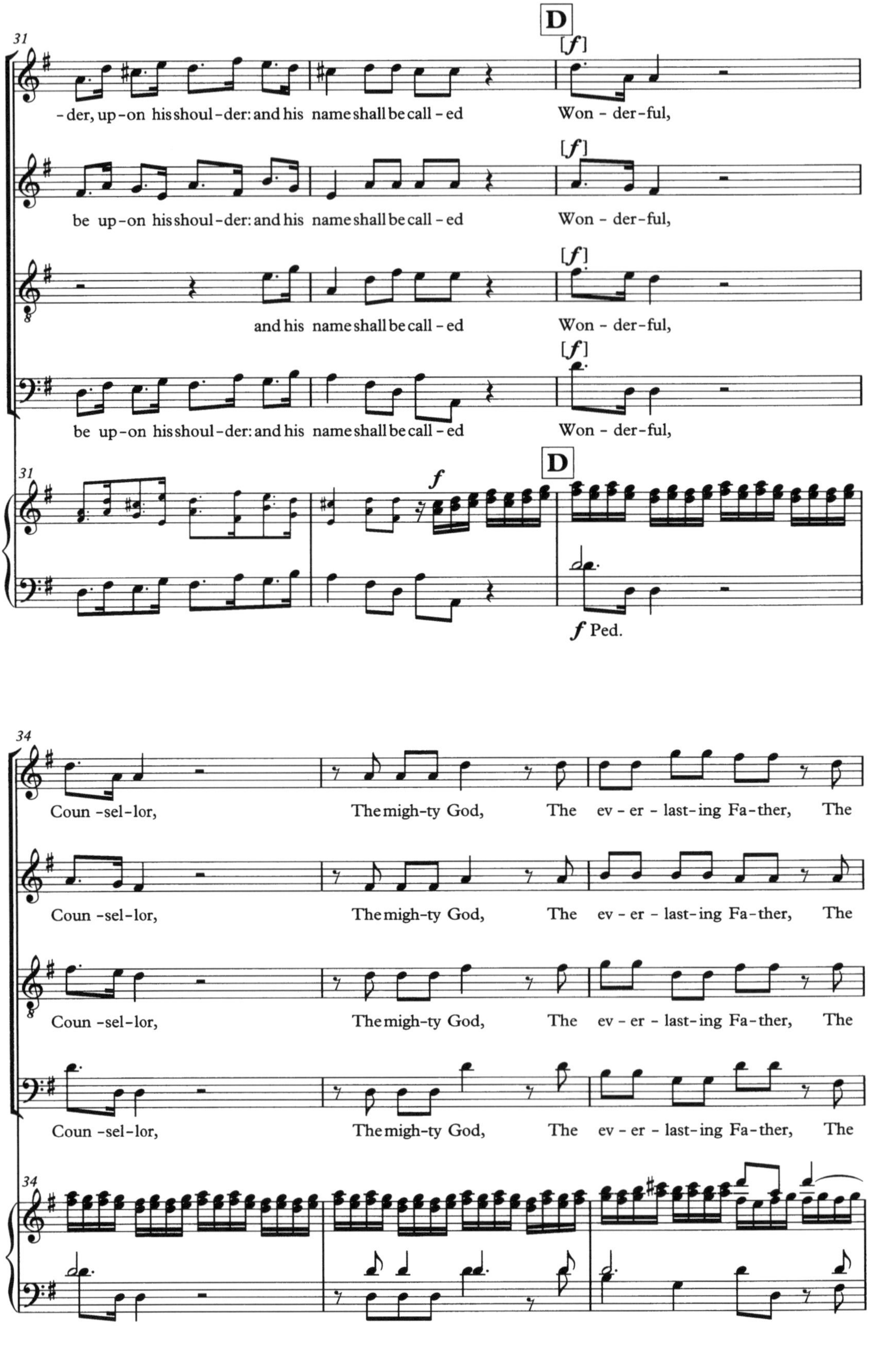

31

D

[*f*]

-der, up-on his shoul-der: and his name shall be call-ed Won-der-ful,

be up-on his shoul-der: and his name shall be call-ed Won-der-ful,

and his name shall be call-ed Won-der-ful,

be up-on his shoul-der: and his name shall be call-ed Won-der-ful,

31

f

D

f Ped.

37
Prince of Peace.
[p]
Prince of Peace. Un - to us a child is born, un - to
[p]
Prince of Peace. For un - to us a child is born,
Prince of Peace.
37
p
p Man.
40
[p]
Un - to us a child is born,
us a son is gi - ven:
[p]
un - to us a son is
40

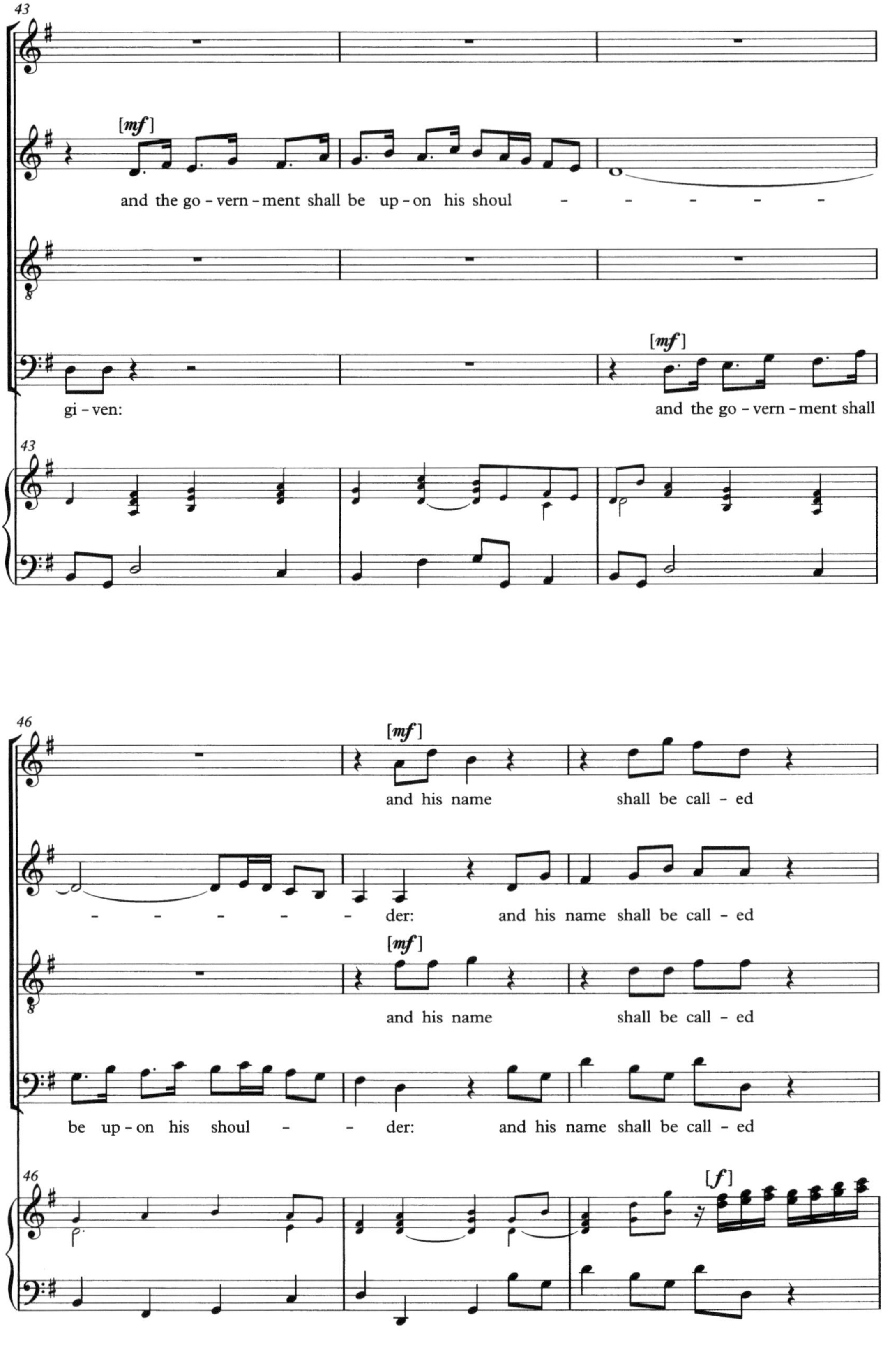

43

[*mf*]

and the go - vern - ment shall be up - on his shoul - - - - - -

gi - ven:

[*mf*]

and the go - vern - ment shall

43

E
49
[f]
Won - der-ful,
Coun - sel-lor,
Won - der-ful,
Coun - sel-lor,
Won - der-ful,
Coun - sel-lor,
Won - der-ful,
Coun - sel-lor,
E
49
[f]
Ped.
51
The migh-ty God, The ev - er - last-ing Fa-ther, The Prince of Peace.
The migh-ty God, The ev - er - last-ing Fa-ther, The Prince of Peace.
[p]
The migh-ty God, The ev - er - last-ing Fa-ther, The Prince of Peace. Un-to
The migh-ty God, The ev - er - last-ing Fa-ther, The Prince of Peace.
51
p Man.

54
[p]
For un - to us a child is born,
[p]
For un - to
us a child is born,
[p]
For un - to us a child is born,
54
p
57
un - to
us a child is born,
un - to
un - to us a son is gi - ven:
57

60
us a son is gi-ven:
us a son is gi-ven: and the go-vern-ment shall be, shall be up-on his
[mf]
60
63
[mf]
and the go-vern-ment shall be, shall be up-on his shoul-der:
[mf]
and the go-vern-ment shall
shoul-der:
[mf]
and the go-vern-ment shall
63

66
F
[f]
and his name shall be call - ed
Won - der-ful,
be up-on his shoul-der: and his name shall be call - ed
Won - der-ful,
and his name shall be call - ed
Won - der-ful,
be up-on his shoul-der: and his name shall be call - ed
Won - der-ful,
[f] Ped.
69
Coun - sel - lor,
The migh-ty God,
The ev - er-last-ing Fa - ther,

72

Prince of Peace. For un-to us a child is born,

Prince of Peace. For un-to us a child is born,

Prince of Peace. For un-to us a child is born, un-to

Prince of Peace. Un-to us a child is born, un-to us a child is born, un-to

72

75

us a son is gi-ven, un-to

us a son is gi-ven, un-to

75

77
un-to us
a son is gi-ven: and the
un-to us
a son is gi-ven:
us a son is gi-ven, un-to us
a son is gi-ven:
us a son is gi-ven, un-to us
a son is gi-ven:
77
80
go - vern-ment, the go - vern-ment shall be up - on his shoul - -
and the go - vern-ment shall be up - on his shoul - der,
and the
and the
80

82
-der, and the go - vern-ment shall be up - on his shoul - der: and his
and the go - vern-ment shall be up - on his shoul - der: and his
go - vern-ment, the go - vern-ment shall be up - on his shoul - der: and his
go - vern-ment, the go - vern-ment shall be up - on his shoul - der: and his
82
84
G
name shall be call-ed Won-der-ful, Coun-sel-lor,
name shall be call-ed Won-der-ful, Coun-sel-lor,
name shall be call-ed Won-der-ful, Coun-sel-lor,
name shall be call-ed Won-der-ful, Coun-sel-lor,
G
84

87
The Migh - ty God, The ev - er - last - ing Fa - ther, The Prince of Peace, The
The Migh - ty God, The ev - er - last - ing Fa - ther, The Prince of Peace, The
The Migh - ty God, The ev - er - last - ing Fa - ther, The Prince of Peace, The
The Migh - ty God, The ev - er - last - ing Fa - ther, The Prince of Peace, The
[tr]
90
ev - er - last - ing Fa - ther, The Prince of Peace.
ev - er - last - ing Fa - ther, The Prince of Peace.
ev - er - last - ing Fa - ther, The Prince of Peace.
ev - er - last - ing Fa - ther, The Prince of Peace.
[tr]
93
96
[tr]

HALLELUJAH

from *Messiah*

Revelation
xix, 6; xi, 15; xix, 16

4

[f]

Hal - le - lu - jah, Hal - le - lu - jah, Hal-le - lu - jah, Hal - le - lu - jah, Hal-

[f]

Hal - le - lu - jah, Hal - le - lu - jah, Hal-le - lu - jah, Hal - le - lu - jah, Hal-

[f]

Hal - le - lu - jah, Hal - le - lu - jah, Hal-le - lu - jah, Hal - le - lu - jah, Hal-

[f]

Hal - le - lu - jah, Hal - le - lu - jah, Hal-le - lu - jah, Hal - le - lu - jah, Hal-

4

7
-le - lu - jah, Hal - le - lu - jah, Hal - le - lu - jah, Hal-le-
-le - lu - jah, Hal - le - lu - jah, Hal - le - lu - jah, Hal-le-
-le - lu - jah, Hal - le - lu - jah, Hal - le - lu - jah, Hal-le-
-le - lu - jah, Hal - le - lu - jah, Hal - le - lu - jah, Hal-le-
7
10
-lu - jah, Hal-le-lu-jah, Hal - le - lu - jah: for the Lord
-lu - jah, Hal-le-lu-jah, Hal - le - lu - jah: for the Lord
-lu - jah, Hal-le-lu-jah, Hal - le - lu - jah: for the Lord
-lu - jah, Hal-le-lu-jah, Hal - le - lu - jah: for the Lord
10

13
A
God om - ni - po - tent reign - eth, Hal-le - lu - jah, Hal-le - lu - jah, Hal-le -
God om - ni - po - tent reign - eth, Hal-le - lu - jah, Hal-le - lu - jah, Hal-le -
God om - ni - po - tent reign - eth, Hal-le - lu - jah, Hal-le - lu - jah, Hal-le -
God om - ni - po - tent reign - eth, Hal-le - lu - jah, Hal-le - lu - jah, Hal-le -
13
A
Tpts.
16
-lu - jah, Hal-le - lu - jah: Hal-le -
-lu - jah, Hal-le - lu - jah: for the Lord God om - ni - po-tent reign - eth, Hal-le -
-lu - jah, Hal-le - lu - jah: for the Lord God om - ni - po-tent reign - eth, Hal-le -
-lu - jah, Hal-le - lu - jah: for the Lord God om - ni - po-tent reign - eth, Hal-le -
16
Tpts.
Str.

20
- lu - jah, Hal - le - lu - jah, Hal - le - lu - jah, Hal - le - lu - jah,
- lu - jah, Hal - le - lu - jah, Hal - le - lu - jah, Hal - le - lu - jah,
- lu - jah, Hal - le - lu - jah, Hal - le - lu - jah, Hal - le - lu - jah,
- lu - jah, Hal - le - lu - jah, Hal - le - lu - jah, Hal - le - lu - jah,
20
Drum solo
22
B
for the Lord God om - ni - - po - tent
Hal - le -
Hal - le - lu - jah, Hal - le - lu - jah, Hal - le - lu - jah, Hal - le -
B
22
Vln. 2

24
reign - - eth, Hal-le - lu - jah, Hal-le - lu - jah, Hal - le - lu -
- lu-jah, Hal-le - lu - jah, Hal-le - lu - jah, Hal-le - lu - jah, Hal - le - lu -
- lu - jah, Hal-le - lu - jah,: for the Lord
Hal-le - lu - jah: for the Lord
24
Tpts.
26
-jah, Hal - le - lu - jah, Hal - le - lu - jah, Hal-le - lu - jah,
-jah, Hal - le - lu - jah, Hal - le - - lu - jah, Hal - le-
God om - ni - - po - tent reign - - eth, Hal-le - lu - jah,
God om - ni - - po - tent reign - - eth, Hal - le-
26

28
Hal-le-lu-jah, Hal-le-lu-jah, Hal-le-lu-jah, Hal-le-lu-jah,
-lu-jah, Hal-le-lu-jah: for the Lord
Hal-le-lu-jah, Hal-le-lu-jah, for the Lord
-lu-jah, Hal-le-lu-jah, Hal-le-lu-jah, Hal-le-
28
Tpts.
Str.
30
Hal-le-lu-jah, Hal-le-lu-jah, Hal - le - lu - jah, Hal -
God om - ni - po - tent reign - - eth, Hal-le-lu-jah,
God om - ni - po - tent reign - - eth, Hal -
-lu-jah, Hal-le-lu-jah, Hal-le - lu-jah, Hal-le - lu-jah, Hal-le-
30
Str.

32
C
[p]
-le - lu - jah. The king-dom of this
Hal - le - lu - jah. The king-dom of this
-le - lu - jah. The king-dom of this
-lu-jah, Hal - le - lu - jah. The king-dom of this
Tpts.
Str.
35
[f]
world is be - come the king - dom of our
world is be - come the king - dom of our
world is be - come the king - dom of our
world is be - come the king - dom of our
Vln.
+ Tpt.

39
D
Lord and of his Christ, and of his Christ;
Lord and of his Christ, and of his Christ;
Lord and of his Christ, and of his Christ;
[f]
Lord and of his Christ, and of his Christ; and he shall
39
Vln.
D
Tpt.
42
[f]
and he shall reign for ev - er and ev -
tr
reign for ev - er and ev - er, for and ev - er, and he shall
42
Str.

46
[f]
and
[f]
[p]
and he shall reign for ev - er and ev - er, for ev - er
-er, and he shall reign for ev - er and ev - er,
reign, and he shall reign for ev - er, for ev - er and ev - er, for
46
49
E
he shall reign for ev - er and ev - - er. KING OF
and ev - er, for ev - er and ev - er. KING OF
and he shall reign_ for ev - er and ev - er,
ev - er and ev - er, for ev - er, for ev - er and ev - er,
49
E

52
KINGS,
AND LORD OF
KINGS,
AND LORD OF
for ev - er and ev - er, Hal - le - lu - jah, Hal - le - lu - jah!
for ev - er and ev - er, Hal - le - lu - jah, Hal - le - lu - jah!
52
Tpts.

55
LORDS,
KING OF
LORDS,
for ev - er and ev - er, Hal le - lu - jah, Hal le - lu - jah!
for ev - er and ev - er, Hal le - lu - jah, Hal le - lu - jah!
55
Tpt.
Str.

58
KINGS,
AND LORD OF
for ev - er and ev - er, Hal-le - lu - jah, Hal-le - lu - jah!
for ev - er and ev - er, Hal-le - lu - jah, Hal-le - lu - jah!
for ev - er and ev - er, Hal-le - lu - jah, Hal-le - lu - jah!
58
61
LORDS,
KING OF
for ev - er and ev - er, Hal-le - lu - jah, Hal-le - lu - jah!
for ev - er and ev - er, Hal-le - lu - jah, Hal-le - lu - jah!
for ev - er and ev - er, Hal-le - lu - jah, Hal-le - lu - jah!
61

64
KINGS,
[ff]
AND LORD OF
for ev - er and ev - er, Hal-le-lu - jah, Hal-le - lu - jah!
for ev - er and ev - er, Hal-le-lu - jah, Hal-le - lu - jah!
for ev - er and ev - er, Hal-le-lu - jah, Hal-le - lu - jah!
64
F
67
LORDS,
AND LORD OF LORDS,
[f]
and he shall
[ff]
KING OF KINGS, AND LORD OF LORDS,
[ff]
KING OF KINGS, AND LORD OF LORDS,
[ff]
KING OF KINGS, AND LORD OF LORDS, and he shall
[f]
F
67
[ff]
Str.
[f]

70
reign,
and he shall reign for
[f]
and he shall reign, and he shall reign for
[f]
and he shall reign, and he shall reign, and he shall reign for
reign for ev - er and ev - er, and he shall
70
Ped.
73
ev - er and ev - er, for ev - er and
ff
ev - er and ev - er, KING OF KINGS, for ev - er and
ff
ev - er and ev - er, KING OF KINGS,
ff
reign for ev - er and ev - er, KING OF KINGS, for ev - er and
73
Tpts.
Str.

* Alto: Handel himself wrote both notes.

82
KINGS, AND LORD OF LORDS, KING OF KINGS, AND LORD OF
KINGS, AND LORD OF___ LORDS, KING OF KINGS, AND LORD OF___
KINGS, AND LORD OF___ LORDS, KING OF KINGS, AND LORD OF___
KINGS, AND LORD OF LORDS, KING OF KINGS, AND LORD OF
82
85
LORDS, and he shall reign for ev - er and ev -
LORDS, and he shall reign for ev - er and ev -
LORDS, and he shall reign for ev - er and ev -
LORDS, and he shall reign for ev - er, for ev - er and ev -
85

88
-er, KING OF KINGS, AND LORD OF LORDS, Hal-le-lu-jah, Hal-le-
-er, for ev-er and ev-er, for ev-er and ev-er, Hal-le-lu-jah, Hal-le-
-er, for ev-er and ev-er, for ev-er and ev-er, Hal-le-lu-jah, Hal-le-
-er, for ev-er and ev-er, for ev-er and ev-er, Hal-le-lu-jah, Hal-le-
88
Tpts.
Str.
91
-lu-jah, Hal-le-lu-jah, Hal-le - lu-jah, Hal - le - lu - jah!
-lu-jah, Hal-le-lu-jah, Hal-le - lu-jah, Hal - le - lu - jah!
-lu-jah, Hal-le-lu-jah, Hal-le - lu-jah, Hal - le - lu - jah!
-lu-jah, Hal-le-lu-jah, Hal-le - lu-jah, Hal - le - lu - jah!
91
Tutti

WORTHY IS THE LAMB THAT WAS SLAIN. AMEN

from *Messiah*

Rev. v, 12-13

9
wis-dom, and strength, and hon-our, and glo-ry, and bless - ing.
wis-dom, and strength, and hon-our, and glo-ry, and bless - ing.
wis-dom, and strength, and hon-our, and glo-ry, and bless - ing.
wis-dom, and strength, and hon-our, and glo-ry, and bless - ing.
9
12
A
Largo
Wor - thy is the Lamb that was slain, and hath re-deem - ed us to
Wor - thy is the Lamb that was slain, and hath re-deem - ed us to
Wor - thy is the Lamb that was slain, and hath re-deem - ed us to
Wor - thy is the Lamb that was slain, and hath re-deem - ed us to
12
A
Largo

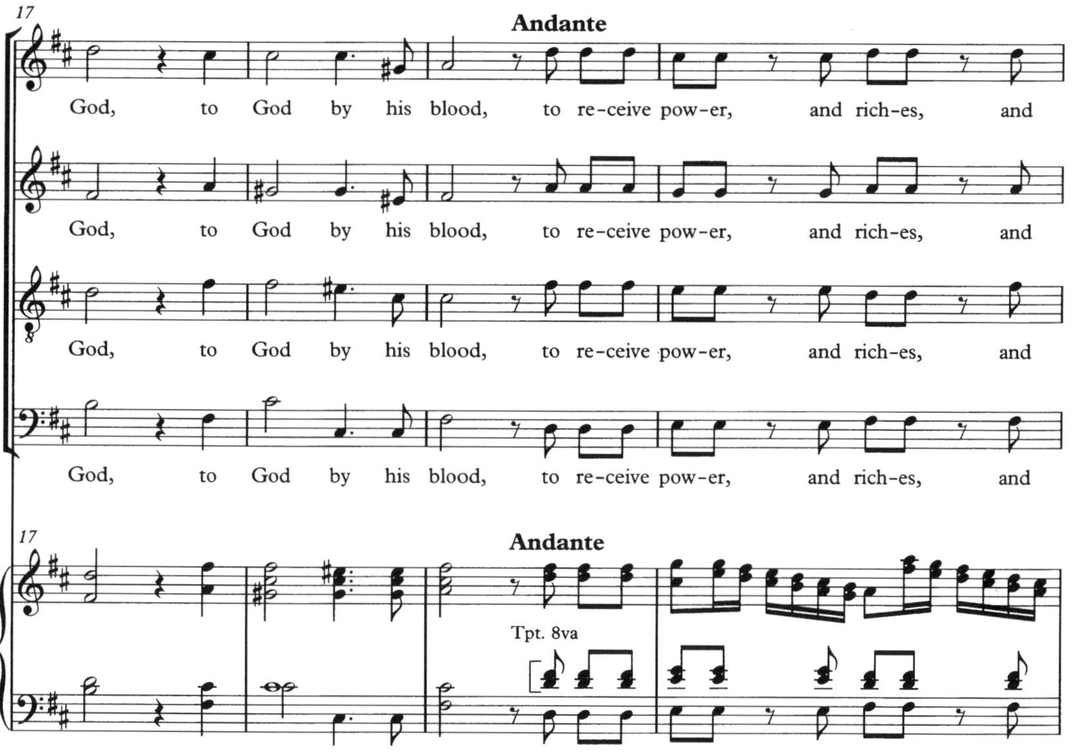
17
Andante
God, to God by his blood, to re-ceive pow-er, and rich-es, and
God, to God by his blood, to re-ceive pow-er, and rich-es, and
God, to God by his blood, to re-ceive pow-er, and rich-es, and
God, to God by his blood, to re-ceive pow-er, and rich-es, and
17
Andante
Tpt. 8va

21
wis-dom, and strength, and hon-our, and glo-ry, and bless - ing.
wis-dom, and strength, and hon-our, and glo-ry, and bless - ing.
wis-dom, and strength, and hon-our, and glo-ry, and bless - ing.
wis-dom, and strength, and hon-our, and glo-ry, and bless - ing.
21

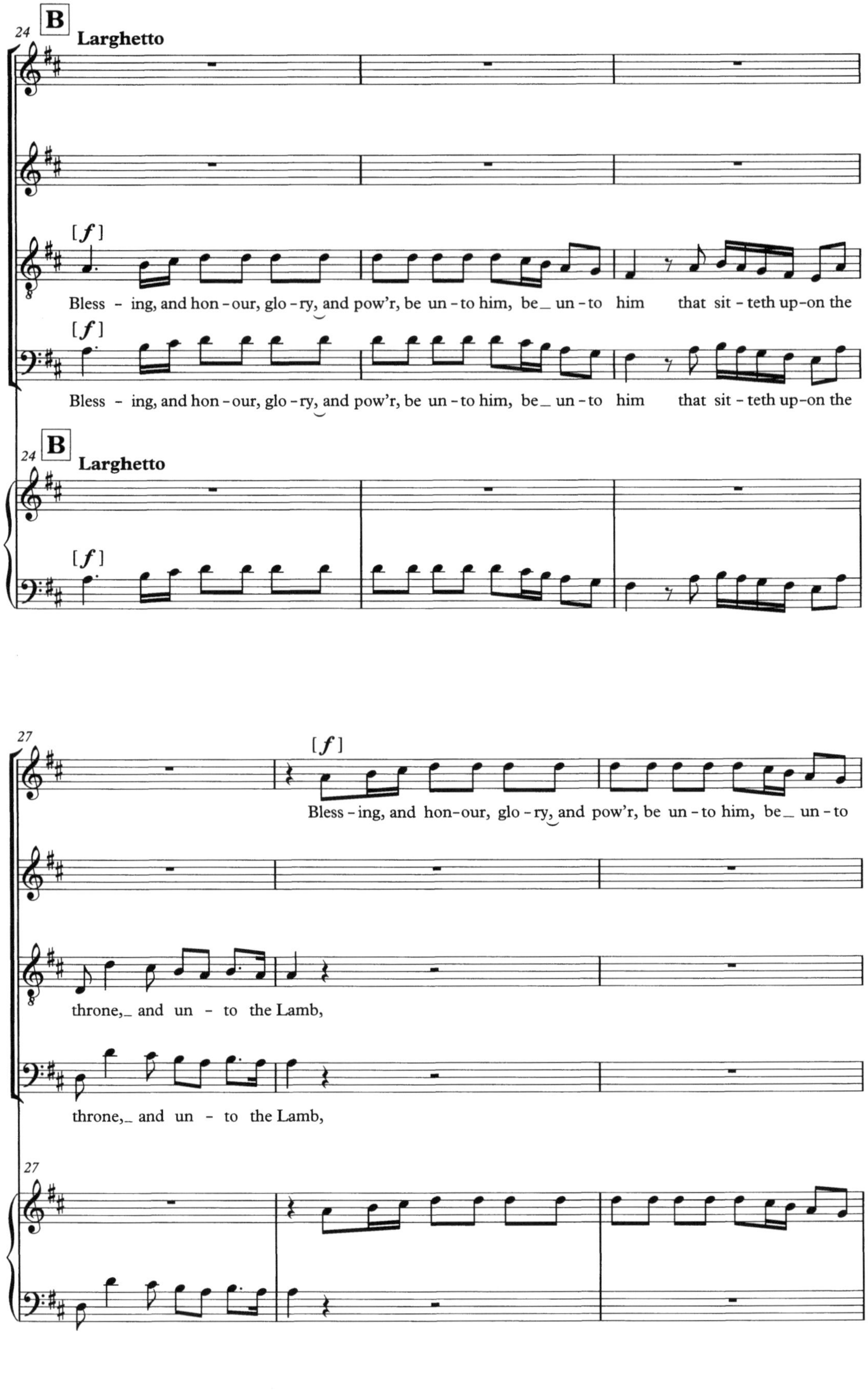

24 **B** **Larghetto**

[*f*]

Bless - ing, and hon - our, glo - ry, and pow'r, be un - to him, be_ un - to him that sit - teth up-on the

[*f*]

Bless - ing, and hon - our, glo - ry, and pow'r, be un - to him, be_ un - to him that sit - teth up-on the

24 **B** **Larghetto**

[*f*]

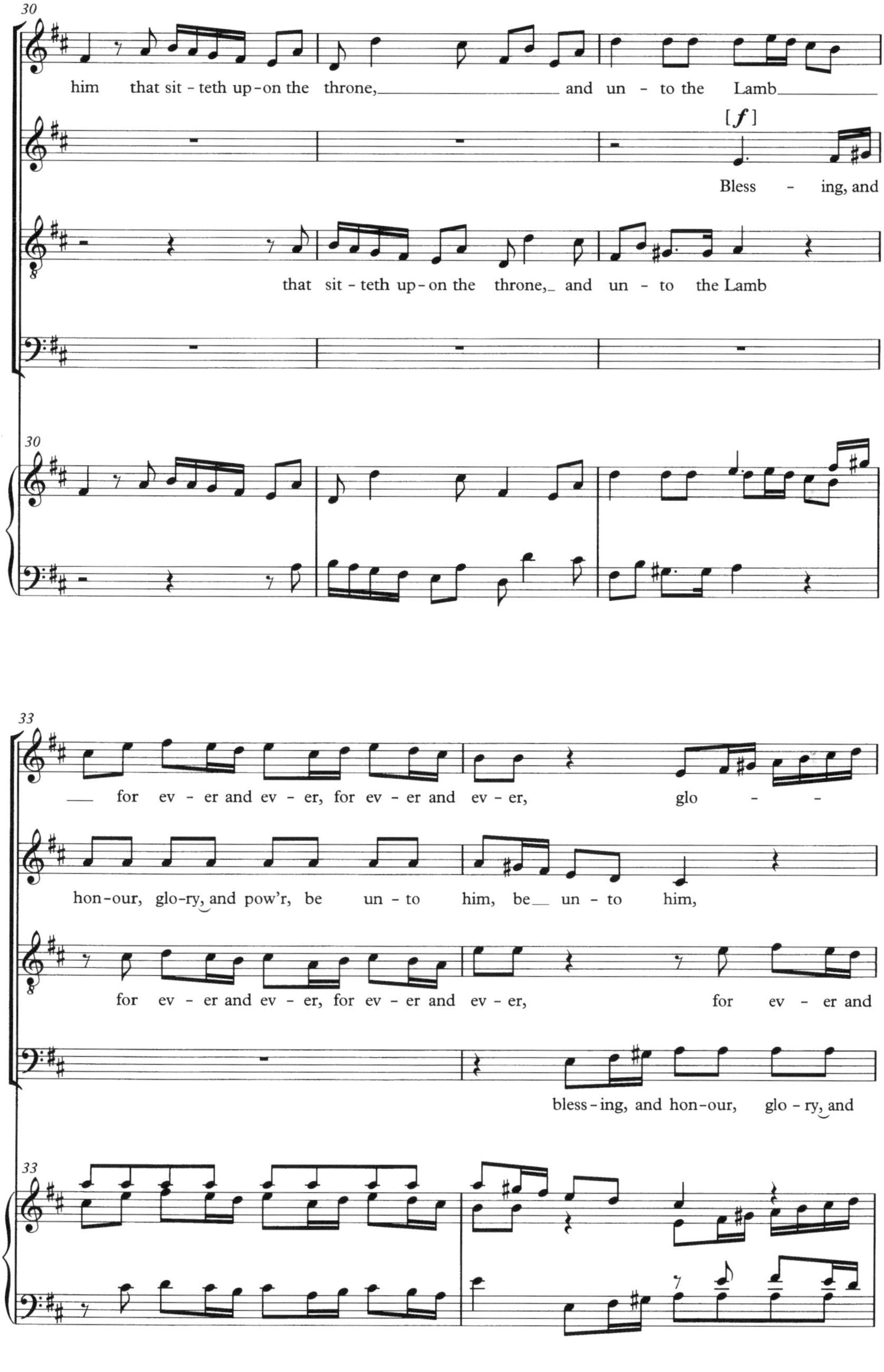

30

him that sit-teth up-on the throne, and un-to the Lamb

[*f*]

Bless - ing, and

that sit-teth up-on the throne, and un-to the Lamb

30

35
– – – – ry,
for - ev - er and ev - er, for ev - er, that
ev - er, for ev - er and ev – – – er,
pow'r, be un - to him, be un - to him that sit - teth up - on the
35
37
that sit - teth up-on the throne, and
sit - teth up-on the throne, up - on the throne, and
and
throne, up - on the throne, up - on the throne, and
37

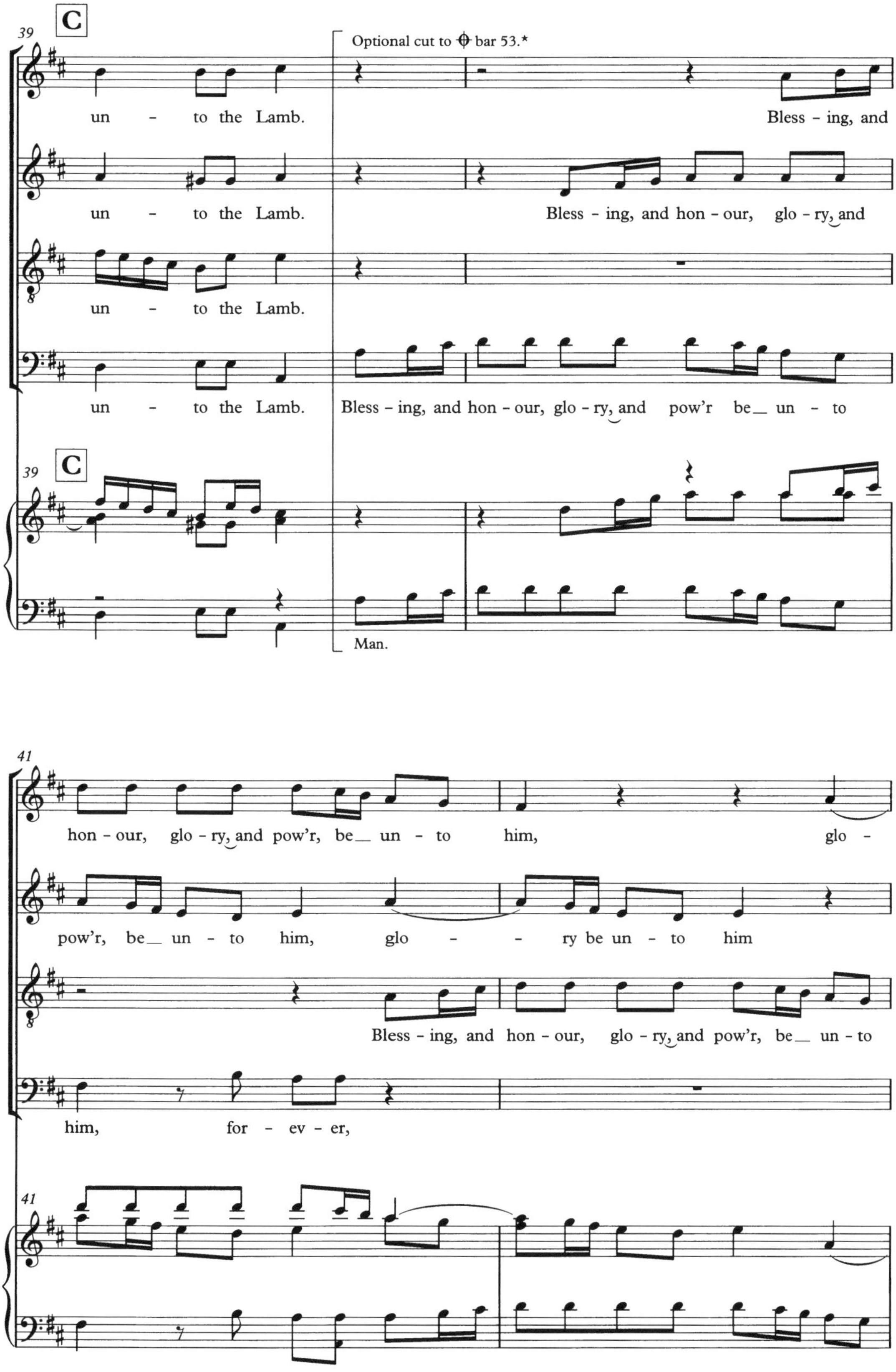

C
39
Optional cut to ⊕ bar 53.*
un - to the Lamb.
Bless - ing, and
un - to the Lamb.
Bless - ing, and hon - our, glo - ry, and
un - to the Lamb.
un - to the Lamb.
Bless - ing, and hon - our, glo - ry, and pow'r be un - to
C
39
Man.
41
hon - our, glo - ry, and pow'r, be un - to him, glo -
pow'r, be un - to him, glo - ry be un - to him
Bless - ing, and hon - our, glo - ry, and pow'r, be un - to
him, for - ev - er,
41

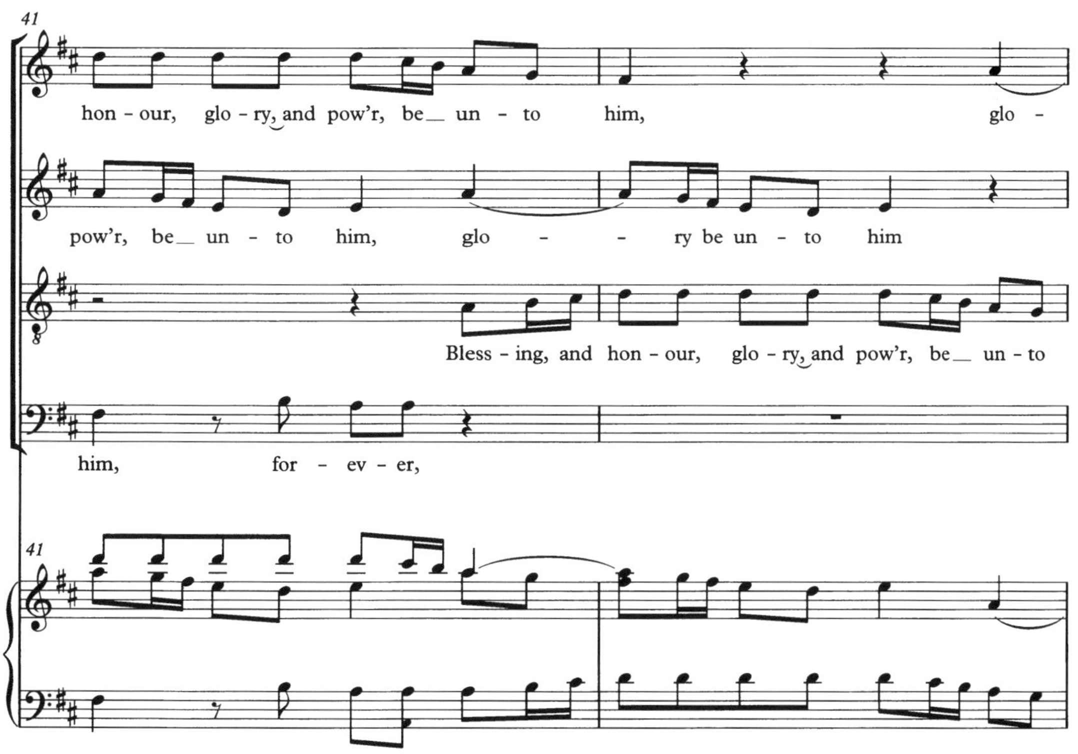

* It has been shown by Donald Burrows that this cut relates to Handel's performance of 1743.

43
- ry be un-to him
that
that sit-teth up-on the throne,
him, and un - to the Lamb,
that sit-teth up-on the throne,
43
46
sit - teth up-on the throne, that sit - teth up-on the throne,
that sit - teth up-on the throne, for
Bless - ing, and
and un - to the Lamb, for
46

48
for_ ev - er and ev - - er, and un -
ev - er and ev - - er, and un -
hon - our, glo-ry, and pow'r, be un - to him, bless - ing, and hon - our, glo - ry, and
ev - er and ev - - er. Bless - ing, and hon - our, glo - ry, and
48
50
-to the Lamb for_ ev - er. Bless-ing, and hon-our, glo-ry, and pow'r, be un-to_
-to the Lamb for_ ev - er. Bless-ing, and hon-our, glo-ry, and pow'r, be un-to
pow'r, be un - to him for ev - er. Bless-ing, and hon-our, glo-ry, and pow'r, be un-to
pow'r, be un - to him for ev - er.
50

53
D
him, be un - to him,
[ff]
him, be un - to him, bless - ing, and hon - our, glo - ry, and pow'r, be un - to
[ff]
him, be un - to him, bless - ing, and hon - our, glo - ry, and pow'r, be un - to
[ff]
bless - ing, and hon - our, glo - ry, and pow'r, be un - to
53
D
[ff]
55
[ff]
blessing, honour, glory, and power, be unto
him, be unto him,
[ff]
blessing, honour, glory, and power, be unto
him, be unto him,
[ff]
blessing, honour, glory, and power, be unto
him, be unto him,
[ff]
blessing, honour, glory, and power, be unto
55
Tpt.
8va

58
him that sit-teth up-on the throne, up - on the throne, and un - to the
him that sit-teth up-on the throne, and un - to the
him that sit-teth up-on the throne, and un - to the
him that sit-teth up-on the throne, and un-to the Lamb, un-to the
58
E
61
Lamb for ev - er, for ev - er and ev - er, for
Lamb for ev - er, for ev - er and ev - er, for ev - er and ev - er, for
Lamb for ev - er, for ev - er and ev - er, for ev - er and ev - er, for
Lamb for ev - er and ev - er, for ev - er and ev - er, for
E
61

64

ev – er and ev – er, for ev – er and ev – er, for ev – er and ev – er, *for* (and)

ev – er and ev – er, for ev – er and ev – er, for ev – er and ev –

ev – er and ev – er, for ev – er and ev – er, for ev – er and ev – er, for

ev – er and ev – er, for ev – er and ev – er, for ev – er and ev –

64

67

Adagio

ev – er, for ev – er and ev – er, for ev – er and ev – er.

– er, for ev – er and ev – er, for ev – er and ev – er.

ev – er, for ev – er and ev – er, for ev – er and ev – er.

– er, for ev – er and ev – er, for ev – er and ev – er.

67 Tpt.

Adagio

[*tr*]

[*attacca*]

F
72
Allegro moderato
[f]
A - - men, A - - - - men, A - - men, A -
F
72
Allegro moderato
[f]
77
[f]
A - - men, A - - - - men, A - - - -
- - men, A - - - - - - men, A - men,
77

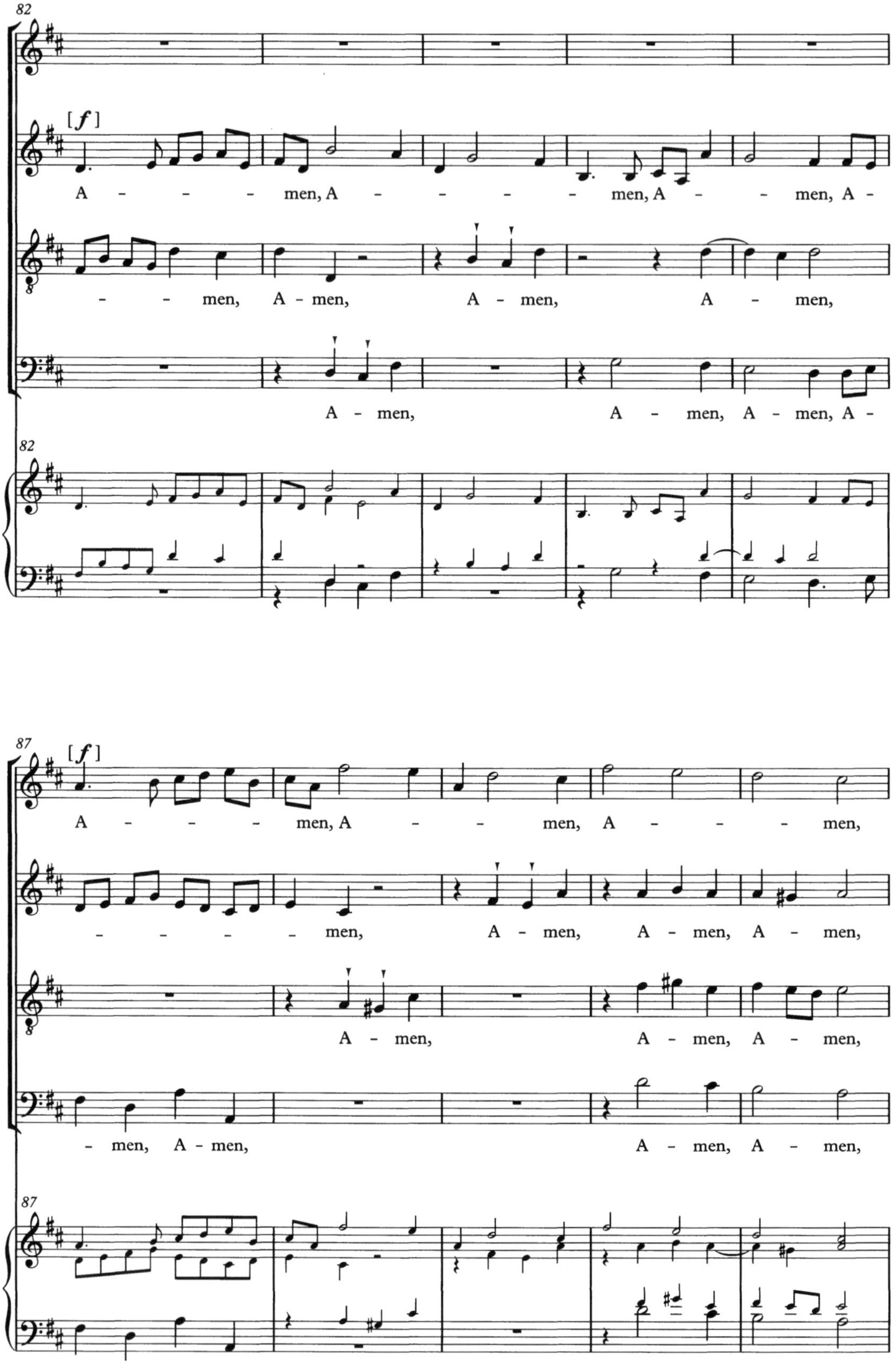

87
[f]
A - - - men, A - - - men, A - - - - men,
- - - - men, A - men, A - men, A - men,
A - men, A - men, A - men,
- men, A - men, A - men, A - men,
87

G

102

[ff]

A – men, A-men, A – men, A – – – – – – men,

[ff]

A – men, A-men, A – – – – – – – – men,

[ff]

A – men, A – men, A – – – – – – men,

[ff]

A – – – men, A – – – – – men, A – men,

102 **G**

[ff]

[f]

107
[ff]
A - - men, A -
[ff]
A - - men,
[ff]
A - - men, A -
[ff]
A - - men, A -
107
[ff]
111
H
[f]
- men, A - - - - men, A - - - - - -
[f]
A - - - - men, A - men, A - - - -
[f]
- - men, A - men, A - men, A - - - - -
[f]
- - - men, A - - - men, A - -
111
H
[f]
f

115
men, A
men, A
men,
men, A
men,
men, A
115
119
I
men,
A
A
men, A
A
men, A
men,
men,
119
I

123

– men, A – – – – – men, A –

– men, A – – – – – – – – – – men, A –

A – – – – – – – – – – – – – men,

A – – men, A –

123

127

– men, A – – – – – –

– men, A – men, A – men, A – – – – –

A – – – – – – – men, A – – – – men,

– men, A – – – – – men A – – men, A –

127

132
K
- men, A - - - - -
- men, A - - - - - - -
A - - - - - men, A - - - - - - -
- - - - - - - - - men, A -
132
K
136
- - - - - - - men, A - men, A - -
- - men, A - - - - men, A - men, A -
- - men, A - - - - - - - men, A -
- - - - - - - - - men, A - men, A - men, A -
136

140
L
men, A - men, A -
men, A - men, A -
men, A - - -
men, A - men, A -
140
L
144
men,
men, A - - men,
[ff]
men, A - men, A - men, A -
[ff]
men, A - -
144
[ff]

148
[ff]
A - - - - men, A - - - - men,
[ff]
A - - men, A - - - men, A - - - - men,
- - - - - - - men, A - men,
- - - - - - - men, A - - men,
148

153
Adagio
A - - - - - men, A - men, A - men.
A - men, A - men, A - men, A - men, A - men.
A - men, A - men, A - men, A - men, A - men.
A - men, A - men, A - men, A - men, A - men.
153
Adagio

LET THE BRIGHT SERAPHIM

from *Samson*

Hamilton after Milton

Bar 9: Handel wrote 'seraphims' at bars 9 and 17, but 'seraphim' at bar 38.

14
an - gel trum - pets_ blow,
17
let the bright Se - ra - phim
in burn - ing row, in
[p]
20
burn - ing, burn - - ing row their loud up - lift - ed an - gel
p
23
tr
trum - pets blow,
their loud up - lift - ed an - gel

26
trum - pets blow
29
their
32
loud,
their loud, up-lift-ed an - gel
35
trum - pets blow.

39
Let the bright Se - ra - phim in burn - ing row, in
[p]
[f]
[p]
42
burn - ing, burn - - ing row their loud, up - lift - ed
46
an - gel trum - pets blow, their loud, up - lift - ed an - gel trum - pets blow,
49
their loud, up - lift - ed an - gel

52
trum - pets blow.
56
Tpt.
59
Let the Che-ru-bic host in tune - ful choirs touch
p
62
their im-mor-tal harps with gold - en wires,
Let the Che-ru-bic host, in

* see p.000

65
tune - ful choirs touch their im-mor-tal harps, touch their im-mor-tal harps
68
with gold - en wires,
71
touch their im-mor-tal harps with gold - en
74
wires.
[f]
segue il coro

The following four bars were composed by Handel for a performance of *Samson* at which bb. 60 - 76 of the Air (or possibly the complete air) were omitted.

LET THEIR CELESTIAL CONCERTS ALL UNITE

from *Samson*

5
e – ver to sound his
e – ver to sound his praise, to sound his praise
5

8
praise, in end - less blaze of light.
to sound his praise
in end – less blaze of light.
8

11
to sound his praise, let their ce-le-stial con-certs
Let their ce-le-stial con-certs
in end-less blaze of light, let their ce-le-stial con-certs
Let their ce-le-stial con-certs
11
f

14
all u-nite, let their ce-le-stial con-certs all u - nite
all u-nite, let their ce-le-stial con-certs all u - nite
all u-nite, let their ce-le-stial con-certs all u - nite
all u-nite, let their ce-le-stial con-certs all u - nite to sound his
14

* Bar 20: All original sources for Handel's oratorio have 'blaze of light' at each occurrence. Milton's text (from *At a Solemn Music*) has 'morn of light'.

23
sound__ his praise in end-less blaze,______ in end - less, end-less blaze of light.
sound his praise in end-less blaze,______ in end-less, end- less_ blaze of light.
sound his praise in end-less blaze of light, in end-less, end-less blaze of light.
sound__ his praise in end-less blaze, in end - less, end-less blaze of light.
23
27
Let their ce-le-stial con-certs all u-nite, let their ce-le-stial con-certs
Let their ce-le-stial con-certs all u - nite,
Let their ce-le-stial con-certs all u-nite to sound his praise______
Let their ce-le-stial con-certs all u-nite,
27

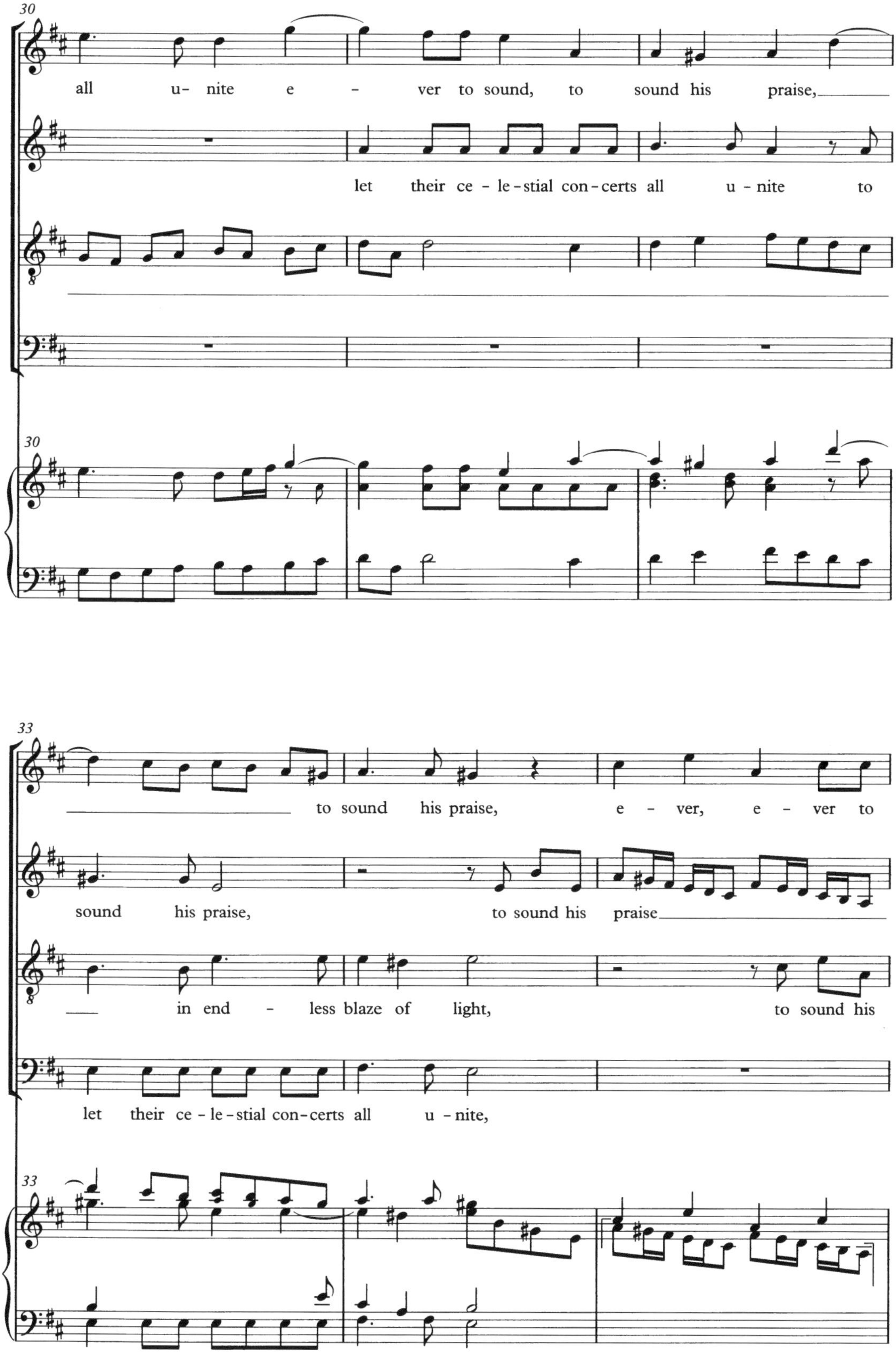

33

to sound his praise, e - ver, e - ver to

sound his praise, to sound his praise

in end - less blaze of light, to sound his

let their ce - le - stial con - certs all u - nite,

33

36

sound his praise in end - - less blaze of light.

— in end - - - - - - less blaze of light.

praise in end-less blaze of light.

e - ver to sound his praise in end-less blaze of light.

36

42
all u - nite
all u - nite
all u - nite e - - - - - - - - ver to
all u - nite e - ver, e - ver, e - ver, e - ver to
42

45
e - ver, e - ver to sound
e - ver to sound his praise in end - less
sound, to sound his praise in end - - less
sound his praise in end - less
45

48
— his praise, e - ver to sound, to sound his praise in
blaze of light, e - ver to sound, to sound his praise in
blaze of light, e - ver to sound, to sound his praise in
blaze of light in end - less blaze, in
48
51
end - less blaze of light, in end - less
end - less blaze of light, in end - less
end - less blaze of light, in end - less
end - less blaze of light, in end - less
51

54
blaze of light.
blaze of light. Let their ce-le-stial con-certs all u-nite
blaze of light. Let their ce-le-stial con-certs all u-nite
blaze of light.
54
58
e - ver to sound, to sound his praise in
e - ver to sound, to sound his praise in
e - ver to sound, to sound his praise in
e - ver_ to sound his praise in
58

61
end - less blaze of light, in end - less
end - less blaze of light, in end - less
end - less blaze of light, in end - less
end - less blaze of light, in end - less
61
64
blaze of light,
blaze of light, Let their ce - le-stial con-certs all u-nite,
blaze of light, Let their ce - le-stial con-certs all u-nite,
blaze of light,
64

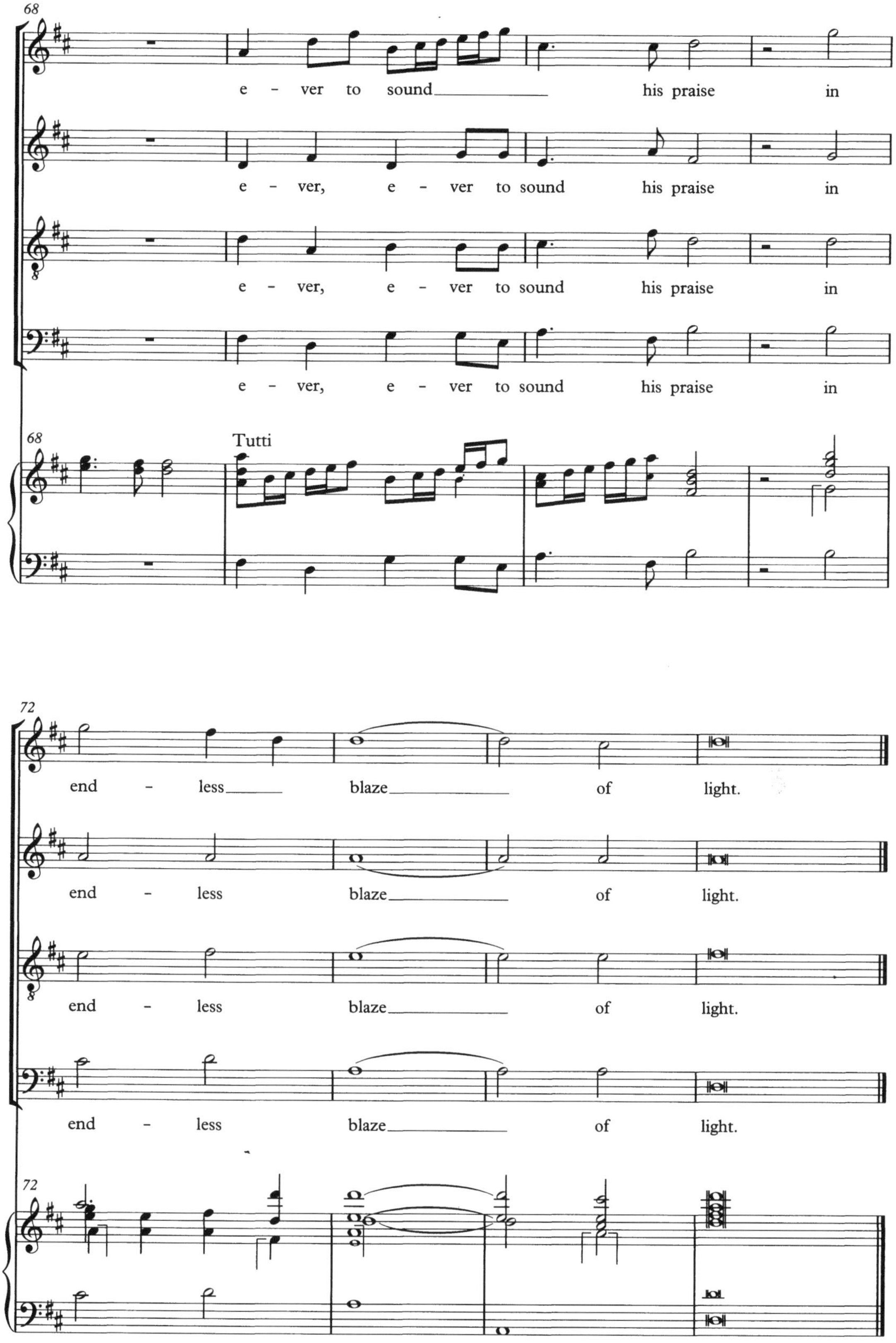

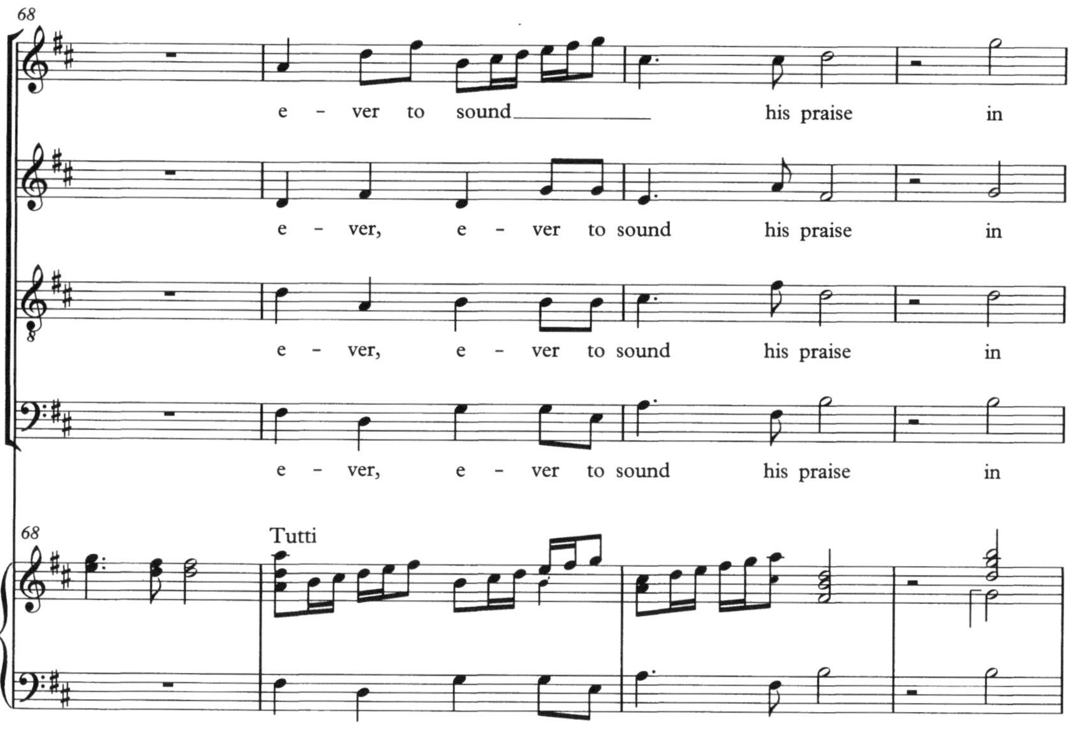

68
e - ver to sound his praise in
e - ver, e - ver to sound his praise in
e - ver, e - ver to sound his praise in
e - ver, e - ver to sound his praise in
68
Tutti
72
end - less blaze of light.
end - less blaze of light.
end - less blaze of light.
end - less blaze of light.
72

HAPPY, HAPPY SHALL WE BE

from *Semele*

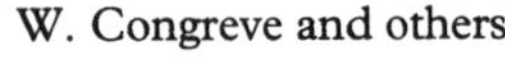

W. Congreve and others

A tempo ordinario

[*f*]

Chorus

SOPRANO [*f*]

Hap - py, hap - py,

ALTO [*f*]

Hap - py, hap - py,

TENOR [*f*]

Hap - py, hap - py,

BASS [*f*]

Hap - py, hap - py,

8

hap - py, hap - py, hap - py, hap - py shall we be,

hap - py, hap - py, hap - py, hap - py shall we be, and free from care, from

hap - py, hap - py, hap - py, hap - py shall we be,

hap - py, hap - py, hap - py, hap - py shall we be,

12
care, from sor - row free, from care, from sor - row free, from
and free from care, from care, from sor - row free, from
and
12

16
and free from care, from care, from
care, from sor - row, from sor - row free, and free from care, from
care, from sor - row free, and free from care, from
free from care, from care, from sor - row free, from care, from
16

20
sor - row free; guilt - less plea - sures we'll en - joy, vir - tuous love will
sor-row free; guilt - less plea - sures we'll en - joy, vir - tuous love will
sor - row free; guilt - less_ plea - sures_ we'll_ en - joy,___ vir - tuous love_ will_
sor-row free; guilt - less_ plea - sures_ we'll_ en - joy,___ vir - tuous love_ will_
20

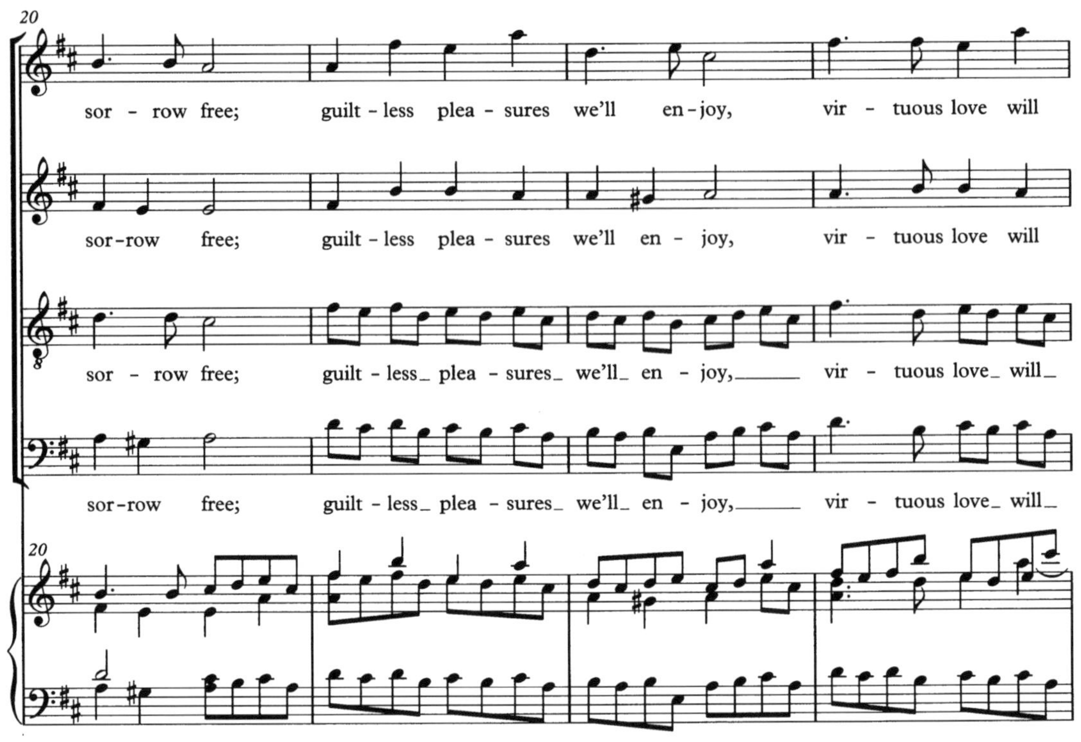

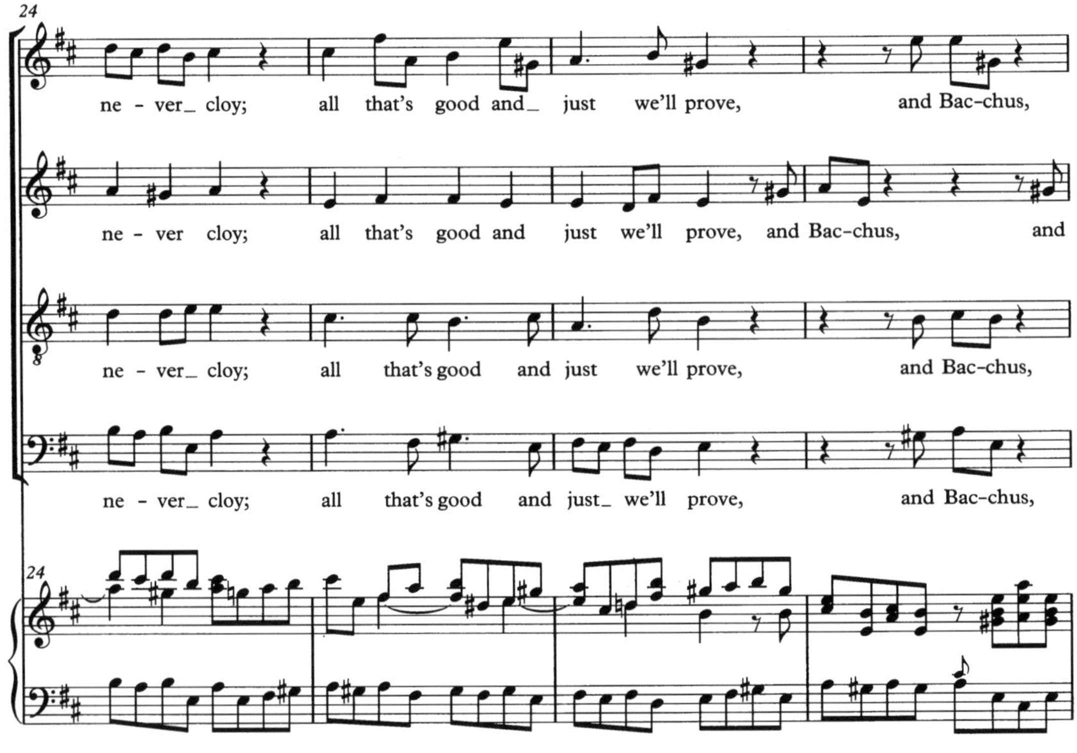

24
ne - ver_ cloy; all that's good and_ just we'll prove, and Bac-chus,
ne - ver cloy; all that's good and just we'll prove, and Bac-chus, and
ne - ver_ cloy; all that's good and just we'll prove, and Bac-chus,
ne - ver_ cloy; all that's good and just_ we'll prove, and Bac-chus,
24

28
and Bac-chus,
and Bac-chus crown the
joys
of
Bac-chus,
and Bac-chus crown the joys
of
love,
the joys
of
and Bac-chus,
and
and Bac-chus,
and
Bac-chus crown the
joys
of
28

31
love,
and Bac-chus crown the
joys
of love,
and Bac
-
chus crown,
love,
of
love,
and Bac-chus crown, crown,
crown,
Bac-chus crown the joys
of
love,
and
Bac-chus crown,
love,
and
Bac-chus crown the
joys,
31

34
crown, crown, crown, crown, crown, and Bac-chus crown the
crown, crown, crown, crown, crown, and Bac - chus crown the
crown, crown, crown, crown, crown, and Bac-chus crown the joys, the
Bac-chus crown the
34
38
joys of love. Hap-py, hap-py,
joys of love. Hap-py, hap-py,
joys of love. Hap-py, hap-py,
joys of love. Hap-py, hap-py,
38

42
hap - py, hap - py, free from care, from
hap - py, hap - py, free from_ care,
hap - py, hap - py,
hap - py, hap - py,
42

46
sor - - row free, from_ care, from sor - row free, and
from sor - - - row free, and
free from care, from sor - - row free, and
free from care, from sor - - row free, and
46

50
Bac-chus, and Bac-chus, and Bac-chus shall_crown the joys of love, the joys of love, and Bac-chus,
Bac-chus, and Bac-chus, and Bac-chus shall_crown the joys of love, the joys of love, and Bac-chus,
Bac-chus, and Bac-chus, and Bac-chus shall_crown the joys of love, the joys of love, and Bac-chus,
Bac-chus, and Bac-chus, and Bac-chus shall_crown the joys of love, the joys of love, and Bac-chus,
50
53
Bac-chus shall_ crown___ the joys of love. Hap - py, hap - py,
Bac-chus shall_ crown the joys of love. Hap - py, hap - py,
Bac-chus shall_ crown___ the joys of love. Hap - py, hap - py,
Bac-chus shall_ crown___ the joys of love. Hap - py, hap - py,
53

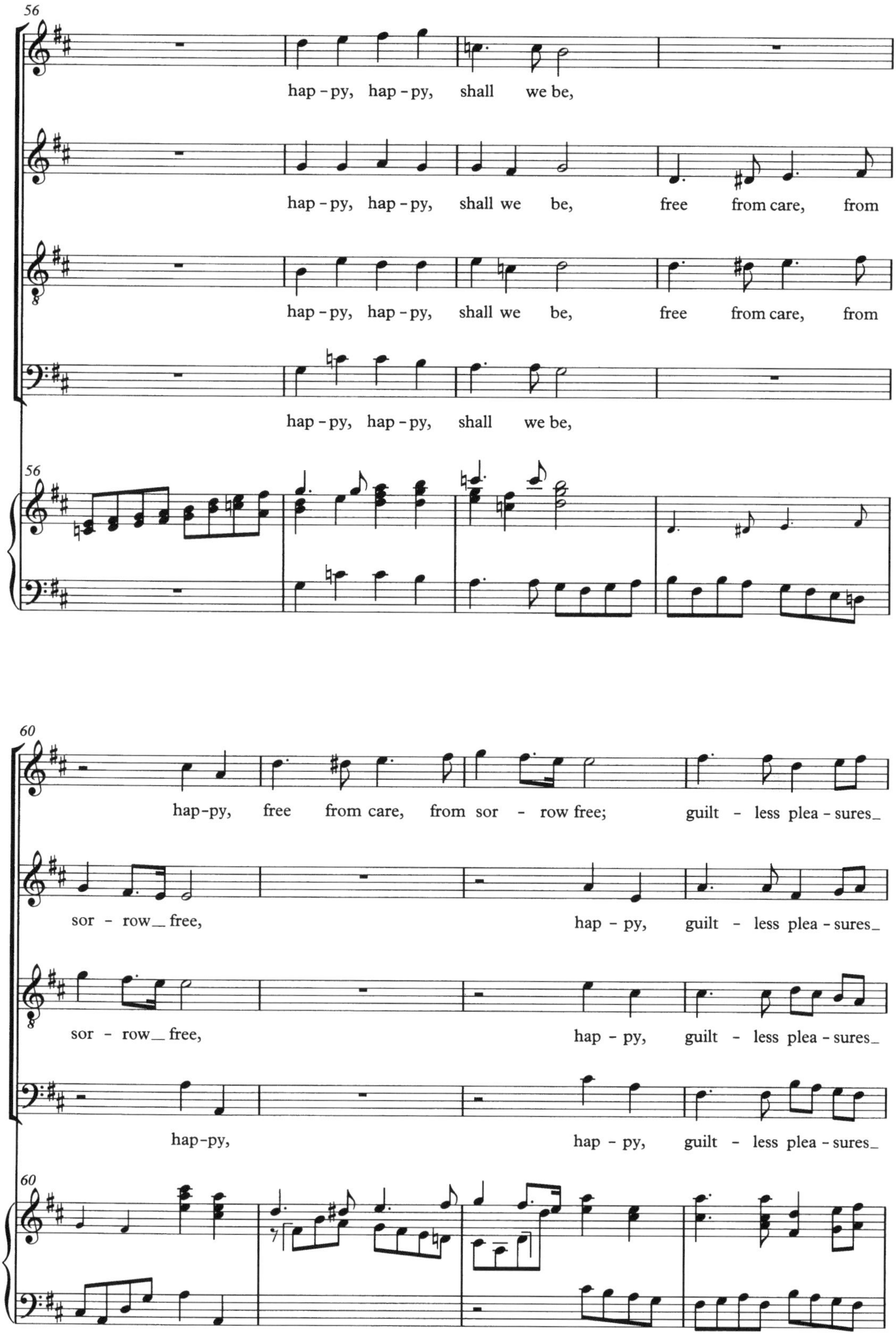

56

hap - py, hap - py, shall we be,

hap - py, hap - py, shall we be, free from care, from

hap - py, hap - py, shall we be, free from care, from

hap - py, hap - py, shall we be,

56

60
hap-py, free from care, from sor - row free; guilt - less plea - sures_
sor - row_ free, hap - py, guilt - less plea - sures_
sor - row_ free, hap - py, guilt - less plea - sures_
hap-py, hap - py, guilt - less plea - sures_
60

64
we'll en - joy, vir - tuous love will ne - ver__ cloy;
we'll__ en - joy, vir - tuous love will ne - ver__ cloy;
we'll en - joy, vir - tuous love will ne - ver__ cloy;
we'll__ en - joy, vir - tuous love will ne - ver__ cloy;
64

67
all that's good and just__ we'll__ prove, and Bac - chus crown the
all that's good and just we'll prove, and Bac-chus, and
all that's good and just__ we'll__ prove, and Bac-chus,
all__ that's__ good and just__ we'll__ prove, and Bac-chus,
67

70
joys of love, and Bac - chus crown, crown, crown the
Bac-chus, and Bac - chus crown, crown, crown the
and Bac-chus, and Bac - chus crown crown, crown the
and Bac-chus, and Bac-chus crown
70
73
joys, the joys of love. Hap-py, hap - py,
joys, the joys of love. Hap-py, hap - py,
joys, the joys of love. Hap-py, hap - py,
the joys of love. Hap-py, hap - py,
73

77
hap - py shall we be, hap - py shall we be, hap - py, hap - py, free from care, from
hap - py shall we be, hap - py shall we be, hap - py, hap - py,
hap - py shall we be, hap - py shall we be, hap - py, hap - py, free from care, from
hap - py shall we be, hap - py shall we be, hap - py, hap - py,
77
81
sor - row free,
and Bac-chus, Bac - chus crown, and
sor - row free, and Bac-chus crown
and Bac-chus crown
81

84
free from care, from sor - row free, and Bac - chus crown the joys of love, and
Bac - chus crown the joys of love, and Bac - chus crown the joys of love, and
the joys of love, and Bac - chus crown the joys of love, and
the joys of love, and Bac - chus crown the joys of love, and
84
88
Bac - chus crown the joys of love.
Bac - chus crown the joys of love.
Bac - chus crown the joys of love.
Bac - chus crown the joys of love.
88

MUSIC, SPREAD THY VOICE AROUND

from *Solomon*

Anon.

18
— mu-sic, spread thy voice a-round,
— mu-sic, spread thy voice a-round,
spread_ thy voice a-round, spread thy voice a-round, mu-sic, spread_ thy
mu-sic, spread thy
spread_ thy voice a-round,
mu-sic, spread_ thy
18
24
mu-sic, spread thy voice a-round, spread thy voice a-
mu-sic, spread thy voice a-round, spread thy voice a-
voice a-round, a-round, mu-sic, spread_ thy voice a-
voice a-round, spread thy voice a-round, mu-sic, spread_ thy voice a-
voice a-round, mu-sic, spread_ thy voice a-
24

* In bb. 40 and 44 (only) Handel wrote sweet - ly

42
flow the lull - ing sound,
flow the lull - ing sound,
flow the lull - ing sound, sweet - ly flow the
sweet - ly,
sweet - ly, sweet - ly flow the lull - ing
42
48
sweet - ly flow the lull - ing
sweet - ly flow the lull - ing
lull - ing sound, the lull - ing sound, flow the lull - ing
sweet - ly flow the lull - ing
sound, the lull - ing sound, sweet - ly flow the lull - ing
48

54
sound,
sweet - ly,
sound,
sweet - ly,
sound,
sweet - ly,
sound,
sweet - ly,
sweet - ly
sound,
sweet - ly,
54
p
[mf]
60
sweet - ly flow the lull - ing sound, the lull - ing sound,
sweet - ly flow the lull - ing sound, the lull - ing sound,
sweet - ly
flow the lull - ing sound, the lull - ing sound, sweet - ly
sweet - ly
60

66
flow the lull - ing sound. Mu - sic spread_ thy voice___ a -
flow the lull - ing sound. Mu - sic spread_ thy voice___ a -
flow the lull - ing sound.
flow the lull - ing sound. Mu - sic, spread_ thy voice___ a -
flow the lull - ing sound.
66
72
-round,_________ mu-sic, spread___ thy voice__ a - round,
-round,_________ mu-sic, spread___ thy voice__ a - round,
Mu - sic, spread_ thy voice__ a - round, spread thy voice a - round, mu - sic,
round, mu - sic,
Mu - sic, spread_ thy voice__ a - round,_________ mu - sic,
72

78

mu - sic, spread__ thy voice__ a - round,________ spread thy

mu - sic, spread__ thy voice__ a - round,________ spread thy

spread__ thy voice__ a - round,______ a - round, mu - sic spread__ thy

spread thy voice______ a - round,_thy voice a - round, mu - sic spread__ thy

spread__ thy voice__ a - round,______ mu - sic spread__ thy

78

84

voice____ a - round, sweet - ly,

voice____ a - round, sweet - ly,

voice__ a - round, sweet - ly flow__ the lull - ing______ sound,

voice a - round, sweet - ly flow__ the lull - ing______ sound,

voice__ a - round, sweet - ly

84

90
sweet - ly flow the lull - ing sound, sweet - ly,
sweet - ly flow the lull - ing sound, sweet - ly,
sweet - ly flow the lull - ing sound,
sweet - ly flow the lull - ing sound,
sweet - ly flow the lull - ing sound,
90
p
96
sweet - ly flow the lull - ing
sweet - ly,
sweet - ly, sweet - ly flow the lull - ing sound, the
sweet - ly,
96

* Handel wrote g''

** Handel wrote ♪♩♩ (lull - ing) (Alto only)

114
sweet - ly flow, sweet - ly flow
spread thy voice a - round; sweet - ly flow
spread thy voice a - round; sweet - ly flow, sweet - ly flow
spread thy voice a - round; sweet - ly flow, sweet - ly flow,
114
120
the lull - ing sound.
the lull - ing sound.
the lull - ing, lull - ing sound.
sweet - ly flow the lull - ing sound.
120
126

PRAISE THE LORD WITH HARP AND TONGUE

from *Solomon*

16
old___ and young; praise the Lord with_ harp and tongue, praise the Lord,
old___ and young; praise the Lord with harp and tongue, praise the Lord,
praise the Lord with_ harp and tongue, praise the Lord,
praise the Lord with harp and tongue, praise the Lord,
16
19
Chorus 1
praise the Lord, praise Him, all ye old and young, ye
praise the Lord, praise Him, all ye old___ and young, ye
praise the Lord, praise Him, all ye old and young, ye
praise the Lord, praise Him, all ye old___ and young, ye
Chorus 2
SOPRANO
Praise the Lord,
ALTO
Praise the Lord,
TENOR
Praise the Lord,
BASS
Praise the Lord,
19

22
old and young, ye old and young, He's in mer - cy
old and young, ye old and young, He's in mer - cy
old and young, ye old and young, He's in mer - cy
old and young, ye old and young, He's in mer - cy
praise the Lord, praise the Lord,
praise the Lord, praise the Lord,
praise the Lord, praise the Lord,
praise the Lord, praise the Lord,
22

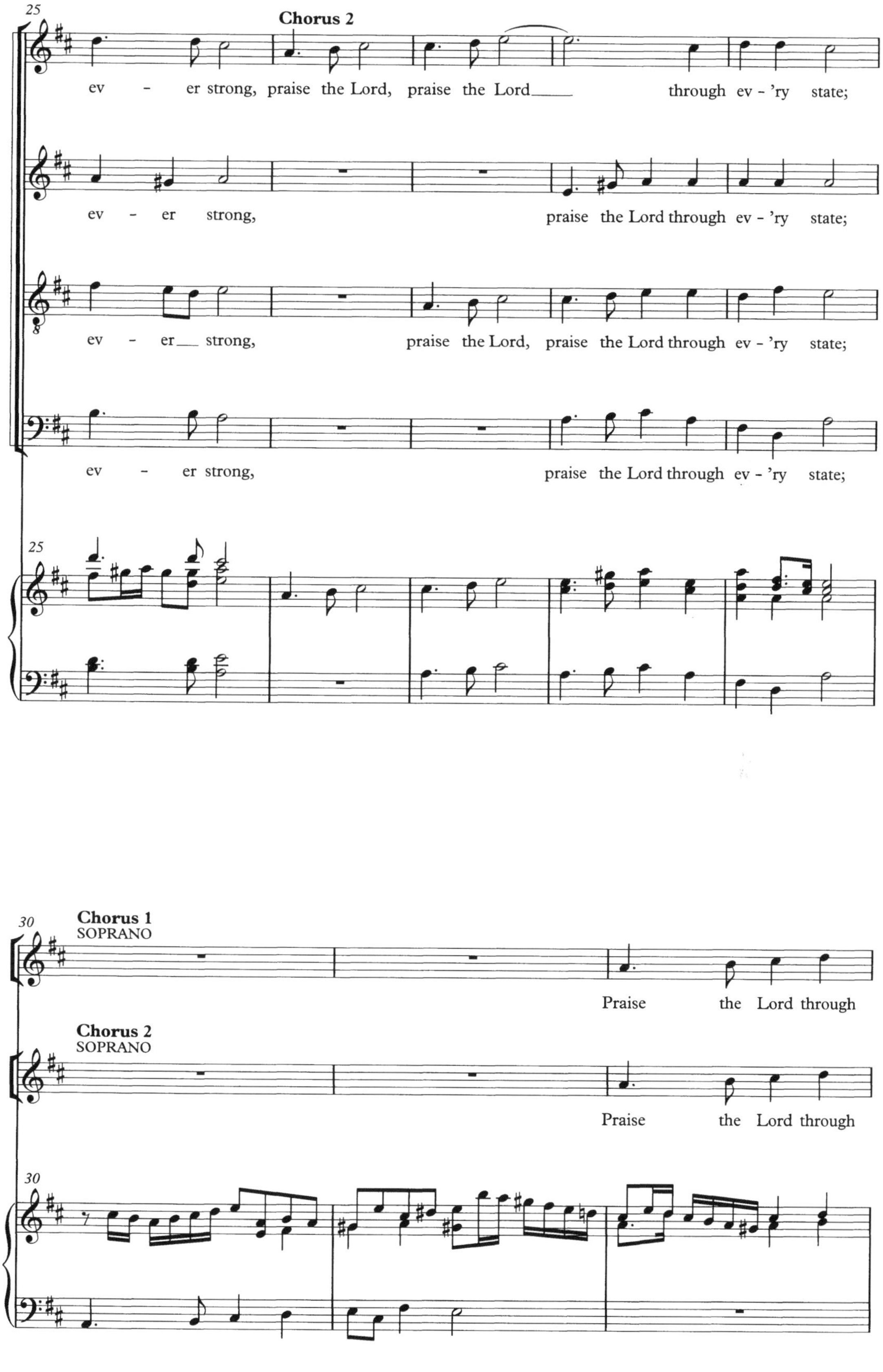

25

Chorus 2

ev – er strong, praise the Lord, praise the Lord____ through ev - 'ry state;

ev – er strong, praise the Lord through ev - 'ry state;

ev – er__ strong, praise the Lord, praise the Lord through ev - 'ry state;

ev – er strong, praise the Lord through ev - 'ry state;

25

33
Chorus 1
ev - 'ry state, praise the Lord, praise the Lord, Praise Him ear - ly,
praise the Lord,
praise the Lord,
praise the Lord,
Chorus 2
ev - 'ry state, praise the Lord, praise the Lord, Praise Him ear - ly,
praise the Lord,
praise the Lord,
praise the Lord,
33
36
Chorus 1
SOPRANO
praise him late,
Chorus 2
praise him late, Praise the Lord through ev-'ry state, praise the Lord,
Praise the Lord through ev-'ry state, praise the Lord,
Praise the Lord through ev-'ry state, praise the Lord,
Praise the Lord through ev-'ry state, praise the Lord,
36

39
praise the Lord,
praise the Lord, praise the Lord,
praise the Lord,
praise the Lord, praise the Lord,
praise the Lord,
praise the Lord, praise the Lord,
praise the Lord,
praise the Lord, praise the Lord,
39
praise the Lord, praise Him ear - ly,
praise the Lord, praise Him ear - ly,
praise the Lord, praise Him ear - ly,
praise the Lord, praise Him ear - ly,
39

42
Chorus 2
Chorus 1 & Chorus 2
praise Him late, praise Him late, God a - lone is
praise Him late, praise Him late, God a - lone is
praise Him late, praise Him late, God a - lone is
praise Him late, praise Him late, God a - lone is
42
45
Chorus 2 only
good and great, God a - lone is good and great,
good and great, God a - lone is good and great,
good and great, God a - lone is good and great,
good and great, God a - lone is good and great,
45

48

Praise the Lord, praise the Lord, He's in mer - cy

Praise the Lord, praise the Lord, He's in mer - cy

Praise the Lord, praise the Lord, He's in mer - cy

Praise the Lord, praise the Lord, He's in mer - cy

Praise the Lord, praise the Lord,

Praise the Lord, praise the Lord,

Praise the Lord, praise the Lord,

Praise the Lord, praise the Lord,

48

51

ev - er strong, praise the Lord,

ev - er strong, praise the Lord,

ev - er strong, praise the Lord,

ev - er strong, praise the Lord,

praise the Lord, Praise him ear - ly,

praise the Lord, Praise him ear - ly,

praise the Lord, Praise him ear - ly,

praise the Lord, Praise him ear - ly,

51

54
He's in mer - cy ev - er strong,
He's in mer - cy ev - er strong,
He's in mer - cy ev - er strong,
He's in mer - cy ev - er strong,
praise Him late, praise Him late,
praise Him late, praise Him late,
praise Him late, praise Him late,
praise Him late, praise Him late,
54
57
praise the Lord, praise the Lord,
ev - er strong, praise the Lord,
praise the Lord, praise the Lord,
praise the Lord, praise the Lord,
God a-lone is good and great, God a-lone is
God a-lone is good and great, God a-lone is
God a-lone is good and great, God a-lone is
God a-lone is good and great, God a-lone is
57

60
Let the loud Ho - san - nas rise,
good and great,
60
63
Wide - ly spread - ing, wide - ly spread - ing
Let the loud Ho - san - nas rise,
63

66
through the skies, through the skies,
through the skies, through the skies,
through the skies, through the skies,
through the skies, through the skies,
Wide - ly spread - ing through the skies,
Wide - ly spread - ing through the skies,
Wide - ly spread - ing through the skies,
Wide - ly spread - ing through the skies,
66
69
wide - ly spread - ing through the skies, through the skies;
wide - ly spread - ing through the skies, wide - ly spread - ing through the skies;
wide - ly spread - ing through the skies, wide - ly spread - ing through the skies;
wide - ly spread - ing through the skies, wide - ly spread - ing through the skies;
wide - ly spread - ing through the skies, wide - ly spread - ing through the skies;
wide - ly spread - ing through the skies, wide - ly spread - ing through the skies;
wide - ly spread - ing through the skies, wide - ly spread - ing through the skies;
through the skies, wide - ly spread - ing through the skies;
69

76
Chorus 2
Chorus 1
Chorus 2
God a - lone, God a - lone, God a - lone,
God a - lone, God a - lone, God a - lone,
God a - lone, God a - lone, God a - lone,
God a - lone, God a - lone, God a - lone,
76

79
Chorus 1
God a - lone is just, God a - lone is
God a - lone is just, God a - lone is
God a - lone is just, God a - lone is
God a - lone is just, God a - lone is
Chorus 2
God a - lone_ is just_ and wise,_ is_ just and_ wise,_
God a - lone is just and wise,_ God a - lone is
God a - lone_ is just and_wise, and wise,_
God a - lone_ is_ just and_ wise,_ God_ a - lone_
79

83
just and wise, God a - lone_ is just_ and wise,
just and wise, God a-lone is just and wise,
just and wise, God a - lone_ is just and_ wise,
just and wise, God a - lone is_ just and_
God a - lone is
wise, God a - lone is
is just and wise, God a - lone is
is just_ and wise, God a - lone is
83

87
is just and wise,
is wise
is just and wise
wise, God a - lone is just and wise
just, God a - lone is just and wise,
just, God a - lone is just and wise,
just, God a - lone is just and wise,
just, God a - lone is just and wise,
87

91
God a - lone,
God a - lone,
God a - lone,
God a - lone,
God a - lone, God a - lone,
God a - lone, God a - lone,
God a - lone, God a - lone,
God a - lone, God a - lone,
91

94

Chorus 1 **Chorus 2** **Chorus 1**

God a - lone, God a - lone, God a - lone,

God a - lone, God a - lone, God a - lone,

God a - lone, God a - lone, God a - lone,

God a - lone, God a - lone, God a - lone,

94

97

Chorus 1 & Chorus 2

God a - lone is just, God a -

God a - lone___ is just___ and wise,___

God a - lone___ is just___ and wise,___

God a - lone___ is___ just and___ wise,___

97

100
-lone is just and wise,
and wise,
is just and wise, and wise,
God a - lone is just and wise,
100
103
Chorus 1
God a - lone is just, God a - lone
God a - lone is just, God a - lone
God a - lone is just, God a - lone
God a - lone is just, God a - lone
Chorus 2
God a - lone is just, God a - lone
God a - lone is just, God a - lone
God a - lone is just, God a - lone
God a - lone is just, God a - lone
103

107
is
just
and
wise.
is
just
and
wise.
is
just
and
wise.
is
just
and
wise.
107
is
just
and
wise.
is
just
and
wise.
is
just
and
wise.
is
just
and
wise.
107

ZADOK THE PRIEST

I Kings i, 39-40

No. 1 Chorus ZADOK THE PRIEST

16
(sim.)
19
A
22
SOPRANO 1
[f]
Za - dok the Priest, and
SOPRANO 2
[f]
Za - dok the Priest, and
ALTO 1
[f]
Za - dok the Priest, and
ALTO 2
[f]
Za - dok the Priest, and
TENOR
[f]
Za - dok the Priest, and
BASS 1
[f]
Za - dok the Priest, and
BASS 2
[f]
Za - dok the Priest, and
22
A + Tpts, Timps
[f]
[Orchestral bass continues in quaver rhythm]

25
Na - than the Pro - phet an - oint - ed
Na - than the Pro - phet an - oint - ed
Na - than the Pro - phet an - oint - ed
Na - than the Pro - phet an - oint - ed
Na - than the Pro - phet an - oint - ed
Na - than the Pro - phet an - oint - ed
Na - than the Pro - phet an - oint - ed
25
28
So - lo - mon King.
So - lo - mon King.
So - lo - mon King.
So - lo - mon King.
So - lo - mon King.
So - lo - mon King.
So - lo - mon King.
28

No. 2 Chorus AND ALL THE PEOPLE REJOIC'D

11
B
-joic'd,
re - joic'd,
re - joic'd,
-joic'd,
re - joic'd,
re - joic'd,
-joic'd,
re - joic'd,
re - joic'd,
-joic'd,
re - joic'd,
re - joic'd,
-joic'd,
re - joic'd,
re - joic'd,
2.
1.
11
B
17
re - joic'd,
re - joic'd,
re -
re - joic'd,
re - joic'd,
re -
re - joic'd,
re - joic'd,
re -
re - joic'd,
re - joic'd,
re -
re - joic'd,
re - joic'd,
re -
2.
17

22
- joic'd, and all the peo - ple re - joic'd,
- joic'd, and all the peo - ple re - joic'd,
- joic'd, and all the peo - ple re - joic'd,
- joic'd, and all the peo - ple re - joic'd,
- joic'd, and all the peo - ple re - joic'd,
1.
2.
22
27
Adagio
re - joic'd, re - joic'd and said:
re - joic'd, re - joic'd and said:
re - joic'd, re - joic'd and said:
re - joic'd, re - joic'd and said:
re - joic'd, re - joic'd and said:
1.
27
Adagio

No. 3 Chorus GOD SAVE THE KING

[f]
men,
a - men, a - men, al - le - lu - ja, a - men,
[cresc.]
[tr]
Vlns, Obs.
Vla., Vc.

C
17
SOPRANO
[f]
God save the King, long live the King. A-men,
ALTO 1
[f]
[tr]
God save the King, long live the King. May the King live for e - ver. A-men,
ALTO 2
[f]
[tr]
God save the King, long live the King. May the King live for e - ver. A-men,
TENOR
[f]
[tr]
God save the King, long live the King. May the King live for e - ver. A-men,
BASS
[f]
God save the King, long live the King. A-men,
C
17
Tutti
[tr]
Vc., Bsns.
Tutti
21
a-men, al - le - lu - ia, al - le - lu - ia, a - men, a - - - - - -
[mf]
a-men, al - le - lu - ia, al - le - lu - ia, a - men, a - - - - - -
[mf]
a-men, al - le - lu - ia, al - le - lu - ia, a - men, a - - - - - -
[mf]
a-men, al - le - lu - ia, al - le - lu - ia, a - men, a - - - - - -
[mf]
a-men, al - le - lu - ia, al - le - lu - ia, a - men, a - - - - - -
21

24
men,
[f]
may the King live,
may the King live,
for
Tutti
Vlns.
27 SOPRANO
e-ver, for e-ver, for e-ver, a-men, a-men, al-le-lu-ia, al-le-lu-ia, a-
ALTO 1
ALTO 2
TENOR
BASS 1
BASS 2
Str., Obs.

30
D
-men, a - - - - - - - - - men,
-men, a - - - - - - - - - men,
-men, a - - - - - - - - - men,
-men, a - - - - - - - - - men,
-men, a - - - - - - - - - men,
-men, a - - - - - - - - - men,
30
D
Tutti
33
SOPRANO
al - le - lu - ia, al - le - lu - ia, a - men, a - men, a - men,
ALTO 1
al - le - lu - ia, al - le - lu - ia, a - men, a - men, a -
ALTO 2
al - le - lu - ia, al - le - lu - ia, a - men, a - men, a - men,
TENOR
al - le - lu - ia, al - le - lu - ia, a - men, a - men, a - men,
BASS
al - le - lu - ia, al - le - lu - ia, a - men, a - men, a - men,
Str., Obs.
33

36
a - men, a - men,
al - le - lu - ia, al - le - lu - ia, al - le - lu - ia, a -
- men, a - men, a - - men, al - le - lu - ia, al - le - lu - ia, al - le - lu - ia, a -
Tutti
39
-men.
Long live the King,
E
Vlns.
Tutti

42
God save the King, long live the King. May the King live,
God save the King, long live the King. May the King live,
God save the King, long live the King. May the King live,
God save the King, long live the King. May the King live,
God save the King, long live the King. May the King live,
42
45
may the King live for e - ver, for e-ver, for e-ver, a-men,
may the King live for e - ver, for e - ver, a-men,
may the King live for e - ver, for e - ver, a-men,
may the King live for e - ver, for e-ver, for e-ver, a-men,
may the King live for e - ver, for e-ver, for e-ver, a-men,
45
Tpt.

48
a-men, al-le-lu-ia, al-le-lu-ia, a-men, a
51
[mf]
F
-men, a-men, a

54
[f]
- - men, a-men, a-men, al-le-lu-ia, a - men, al-le-
57
Adagio
-lu-ia, a-men, a-men, al-le-lu-ia, al-le-lu-ia.
Tpts.

NOVELLO REVISED STANDARD CHORAL EDITIONS

Fully revised and edited performing versions of many of the major works in the large-scale choral concert repertoire, replacing the standard Novello editions, often putting back the composers' intentions, restoring the original text, modernised accompaniments and providing new English translations.
Orchestral material, where necessary, is available on hire.

J.S. BACH
(ed. Neil Jenkins)

Christmas Oratorio
NOV072500
German and English text

Magnificats in D & E♭
NOV072529
German and English text in the four Lauds in the E♭ version

Mass in B minor NOV078430

St. John Passion
NOV072489
German and English text

St. Matthew Passion
NOV072478
German and English text

BEETHOVEN
(ed. Michael Pilkington)

Choral Finale to the Ninth Symphony
NOV072490
German and English text

Mass in C
NOV078560

Missa Solemnis (Mass in D)
NOV072497

BRAHMS
(Pilkington)

A German Requiem
NOV072492
German and English text

DVOŘÁK
(Pilkington)

Mass in D NOV072491

Requiem NOV072516

Stabat Mater NOV072503

Te Deum NOV078573

ELGAR
(ed. Bruce Wood)

The Dream of Gerontius
NOV072530

Great Is the Lord
NOV078595

GOUNOD
(Pilkington)

Messe solennelle de Sainte Cécile
NOV072495

HANDEL

Belshazzar
(ed. Donald Burrows) NOV070530

Four Coronation Anthems
NOV072507
The King Shall Rejoice
(ed. Damian Cranmer)
Let Thy Hand be Strengthened
(Burrows)
My Heart is Inditing *(Burrows)*
Zadok the Priest *(Burrows)*

Judas Maccabaeus
(ed. Merlin Channon)
NOV072486

The King Shall Rejoice
(Cranmer) NOV072496

Messiah
(ed. Watkins Shaw) NOV070137
Study Score NOV890031

O Praise the Lord (from Chandos Anthem No. 9)
(ed. Grayston Beeks) NOV072511

This Is the Day
(ed. Hurley) NOV072510

Zadok the Priest
(Burrows) NOV290704

HAYDN
(ed. Pilkington)

The Creation
NOV072485
German and English text

The Seasons
NOV072493
German and English text

Te Deum Laudamus
NOV078463

"Maria Theresa" Mass
NOV078474

Mass "In Time of War"
NOV072514

"Nelson" Mass
NOV072513

Harmoniemesse
NOV078507

MAUNDER

Olivet to Calvary
NOV072487

MENDELSSOHN
(Pilkington)

Elijah
NOV070201
German and English text

Hymn of Praise
NOV072506

MOZART

Requiem
(ed. Duncan Druce) NOV070529

Coronation Mass (Mass in C K.317)
(Pilkington) NOV072505

Mass in C minor
(reconstr. Philip Wilby) NOV078452

PURCELL

Come, Ye Sons of Art, Away
(Wood) NOV072467

Welcome to All the Pleasures
(Wood) NOV290674

Ed. Vol. 15 Royal Welcome Songs 1
(Wood) NOV151102

Ed. Vol. 22A Catches
(ed. Ian Spink) NOV151103

ROSSINI
(Pilkington)

Petite messe solennelle
NOV072436

SCHUBERT

Mass in G, D.167 (SSA version)
NOV070258

SCHÜTZ
(Jenkins)

Christmas Story
NOV072525
German and English text

STAINER
(ed. Pilkington)

The Crucifixion
NOV072488

VERDI
(Pilkington)

Requiem
NOV072403

VIVALDI
(ed. Jasmin Cameron)

Gloria
NOV078441